East Jordan
REMEMBERS

A COLLECTION OF STORIES ABOUT EAST JORDAN'S PAST

EDITED BY
Joan Sheridan Hoover, Jody Malpass Clark and David L. Knight

PUBLISHED FOR THE
Portside Art and Historical Museum Society
East Jordan, Michigan

WITH SUPPORT FROM THE
East Jordan Area Chamber of Commerce

Published by

 HARBOR HOUSE
PUBLISHERS

Harbor House Publishers, Inc., 221 Water Street, Boyne City, Michigan 49712

Manufactured in the United States of America

Hoover, Joan Sheridan 1957- ; Clark, Jody Malpass 1943- ; Knight, David L. 1951-

EAST JORDAN REMEMBERS

A collection of stories about East Jordan's Past

ISBN 0-937360-39-2

Table of Contents

George Secord, 1909-1994

A Note from the Editors

East Jordan Remembers: A Collection of Stories about East Jordan's Past represents a collaborative effort between the Portside Art and Historical Museum Society and the East Jordan Area Chamber of Commerce. The book is dedicated to the memory of George Secord who was devoted to preserving the historical record and sharing his wealth of knowledge about local history.

This work is a "narrative history." We did not attempt to produce a comprehensive history of the community, as much as an anthology of stories about people, things and events that, taken together, form a colorful mosaic of East Jordan's past. Many stories in this collection were drawn from personal experience and may have been lost to future generations if not for this project.

Stories were solicited at large. They came from area natives, long time residents, people with family ties to East Jordan and even people new to the community. Such breadth of authorship helped make the project a true community effort. It also reflects the sense of pride that has had so much to do with shaping the personality of East Jordan.

The volume of material submitted for the book far exceeded that which could be included. All contributions were kept on file, however, and can be accessed at the Portside Art and Historical Museum at Elm Pointe. Anyone wishing to learn more about the history of East Jordan is encouraged to use this excellent resource for further study.

We wish to thank everyone who helped produce this book including the story authors, project volunteers and financial contributors. We hope it is enjoyed and shared with a friend—just as any good story should be.

Jody Malpass Clark
Joan Sheridan Hoover
David L. Knight

Pioneer days:
A history of early East Jordan

BY GEORGE SECORD

Editors' note: George Secord and his mother, Mabel, are responsible for much of the recorded history that exists about East Jordan. This particular account has been widely circulated among George's friends and fellow history buffs. Some of the stories included in this brief history appear in more detail elsewhere in this book.

When the Secords began collecting data on East Jordan during the 1920s, many of the first generation settlers were not only still living but still active in the community. Other sources of information have included "The Traverse Region," published in 1884 and "History of Northern Michigan," Volume 1, by P. Powers (Chicago 1912).

Before the Europeans came to the region it was populated by Native Americans. Bands of Ottawa Indians would encamp from time to time near the mouth of what is now the Jordan River. John Kenny and Robert Webster stated that a couple of times a group would build an oblong structure about 30 feet in length and spend the winter there. Lachlan McLean also told of it.

In any conversation dealing with the early days of what became East Jordan, certain names stand out: George W. Esterly, Solomon Isaman, Lachlan McLean, John Munro (later spelled "Munroe" and still later "Monroe"), John Nichols, David Parrish, Andrew Struthers and Amos Williams. These men all arrived by the early 1860s. Munro is remembered by Monroe Creek and also the Rogers Bridge, which was originally called the Munro Bridge since Munro built the dam spillway just south of it.

Esterly, Nichols and Williams are remembered by the names of East Jordan streets. Moreover, Williams, who was an old time Methodist circuit rider, should be best remembered for giving the Jordan River its name. According to Parrish, who poled the river for many years, Amos built a bark canoe (others said it was a pine log dugout) which he called The Good Ship Zion.

He "squatted" on some land along the west shore of the South Arm about two miles from the head of the lake. But when the Grand Rapids & Indiana Railroad received it's government land grant on February 14, 1857, Williams found he was on railroad land and moved to another location. Amos was still around the area in 1862, then he disappeared and never returned. Some people felt, with the Civil War in full stride, that the old Methodist rider may have enlisted in the Union army as a chaplain.

At the time Williams had his canoe Zion, there were three other boats on the lake. One similar to the Zion was built by Hugh Miller and named the Leviathan. Samuel Horton had one called the Rover and an old gentleman by the name of Holland had a sailboat which bore the grandiose name of Bucephalus. These four craft comprised the Pine Lake fleet.

East Jordan has always been a town which seems to enjoy bucking tradition. Contrary to the procedure in most places, it grew from west to east, developing many roots before it eventually became a town. When that time arrived it was the United States Post Office Department in Washington that selected and gave it the name East Jordan.

With the close of the Civil War many people started coming into the area and taking up government claims. From 1867 through 1870, settlers included the Kenny and LaLonde families, Dave and Robert Shepard, Benjamin Rogers and George Whitfield. Bohemian and Moravian families were homesteading in the "Bohemian Settlement," most having come from around Prague.

Among those who came to the area was Solomon G. Isaman who arrived in 1866 and, in the spring of 1867, located on an 80-acre tract on the west side of Pine Lake in what later would become part of South Arm township.

The original town, Nelsonville, was located at what has always been known as Nettleton's corners, now the intersection of M-66 and Erie Street/Nelson Road. A post office was established there in 1869 with David C. Nettleton as postmaster.

This undated depiction shows the property of Solomon G. Isaman, one of the first merchants in what was then the village of South Arm. *Photo from the collection of William Huckle.*

Meanwhile, things were taking place along the west shore. Isaman built a fair-sized log cabin near the intersection of Jordan and W. Water Streets. In 1870 he married Miss Minnie Czinkus and about 1873 began his mercantile business. His stock consisted of a few staple articles in a corner of his home. On November 23, 1874, the Nelsonville post office was moved to his store, the name was changed to South Arm, and he was made postmaster, a position he held until 1877.

W. Fletcher Empey arrived in 1874 and bought some land from Isaman to build South Arm's first commercial building. In 1876 Henry B. Stohlman came to South Arm and, in partnership with E. A. H. Cole, started a mercantile business. Later in 1882 Cole would withdraw from the partnership and construct the Eagle hotel on the corner of Bridge and W. Water. Both Cole and Stohlman served terms as South Arm postmaster.

Across from South Arm on the east shore of the lake the Nichols Lumber Company built a log cabin in the early 1860s to house any of their men having to spend the night in the area. This was the only building on the east side until 1867 when the Jesse Weikel family settled on an 80 acre tract across from Sunset Hill later known as the Winters farm.

They entertained travellers in their home for several years. Then, in 1877 Weikel built a small inn further south. This, along with several additions, became the Jordan River House. It was destined to go through a number of name changes over the years. Under other managements it became the Central House, the Waverly, the Hotel Lakeside and, finally, the Russel House. It was razed in 1940.

Near the Nichols building, Joseph Maddock built a blacksmith shop, small house and barn. Later, the house was turned around, moved a few feet east, and eventually became the Gothro barber shop. Maddock married the widow Mrs. Alexander who had six children. To put it mildly, the small house was somewhat taxed for space.

In 1876 Empey decided to set up a business on the east shore across from South Arm. He build a small store on the northwest corner of Main and Mill. Next to it was a little shooting gallery and peanut stand operated by Al Pickard.

The first school was a log structure measuring 24 by 16 feet with a seven foot ceiling across the street from what became Sunset Hill cemetery. It opened as Mayhew No. 1 in December of 1877, with Elizabeth Whitfield as teacher earning $20 per month. Many of her first students later became prominent in East Jordan. The first class had six Alexanders (the step-children of Joseph Maddock)—Charlie, Eddie, Isabell, Margaret Jane, Maria and William; George and Willie Mayhew; Anthony, Johnnie and Mary Kenny; Augusta, Eliza, Mary and Mitchell LaLonde; Freddie, Georgie and Johnny Miller; Thomas Bowen; Charley Fresee; Mattie Holben; Anna Keat; Jacob Keller; Josie Swanson; Alonzo and another Hogan; Minnie and another Mitchell; three Allen children; and three Bushnell children. Several years later, Jacob Keller would sell the property across from the school to East Jordan for a cemetery.

Many years later Lillian Isaman Brabant retained a vivid memory of a day she spent in that school. Although too young to attend, she wanted to visit so the Alexander children offered to take her with them. On the designated morning her father rowed her across the lake. At the Maddock house she laid her lunch down outside and when it came time to leave for school, they found that the Maddock pigs had eaten her lunch. She said, "I cried, but Mrs. Maddock laughed and packed me a nice dinner and I skipped off happily with the others for my first glimpse of the inside of a school room. However, I had the last laugh on those pigs. Mr. Maddock butchered them that fall and my father bought one—so I got my lunch back."

In 1878, Sol Isaman donated land for South Arm's

Soloman Isaman. *Photo from the Portside Art and Historical Museum collection.*

first school. It was a two-story frame building and stood on what is now the southeast corner of M-32 and M-66. It opened in 1879 with Alice Glenn teaching the younger children on the upper floor and Mary Cooper of Charlevoix teaching the older ones downstairs. The school board consisted of Sol Isaman, Judge James Keaton, and Henry Stohlman.

In the mid-1860s, Father Zorn would come from Little Traverse (now Harbor Springs) and conduct Catholic services in the various homes. A small Catholic church was built in East Jordan in 1879 with Father Gustav Graf as permanent priest. In the early 1880s Methodist services were being held in South Arm, the people meeting in various homes.

In 1879, Joseph C. Glenn brought the Glenn and Porter sawmill from Leland and set it up at the south end of Main Street. It became Mill "A." This marked the beginnings of East Jordan as an industrial center. About this same time John Nichols built a three-story frame building just north of the present bowling alley. It housed the H. L. Page hardware store with Ed Hodges as first manager. The next owner was Wm. H. Healey who, in turn, sold it to Albert F. Bridge of Charlevoix. Later Bridge sold it to W. E. Malpass and it became the Malpass Hardware Company with Charles Malpass operating it.

The building was razed about 1940. In 1880 there was a beautiful stand of white pine trees on the southwest corner of Esterly and Main. Across Esterly, starting where the Masonic Temple stands, north to the area occupied by Hite's drug store, Rheul Chaddock started construction of a large hotel, the Chaddock House. However, before being completed, he sold it to

Dan Jerrue who completed the three-story building and renamed it the Commercial House.

Jerrue then bought the southwest corner, including the pine grove, from Maggie Coulter, with the understanding he would build a hardware store. But he instead built a large two-story building housing East Jordan's first saloon on the main floor and a dance hall above.

1882 was "boom" year for the young town. A second school was built in town replacing the log one. By now Main and Mill streets were filling with buildings and it was deemed time to bring the two villages closer together, so John Monroe was hired to build a piling bridge connecting East Jordan and South Arm.

E. N. Clink purchased the Boyne City Enterprise in April 1882 and moved it to East Jordan renaming it the East Jordan Enterprise. After several changes in ownership it was bought by C. L. Lorraine in 1890 who, with his sons Bert and Roy, continued to publish it. Later Bert took sole ownership and continued publication until the final issue of its 39 year existence.

The Presbyterian church was organized in 1882 under the direction of Reverend John Redpath of Boyne Falls and Reverend James Lamb. The present church was built in 1883. That year also saw the establishment of the East Jordan Iron Works.

Many of the old land abstracts contain the words "Village of South Lake." In the book "The Traverse Region," published in 1884, there is an account of an 1883 initiative to incorporate the village as South Lake. However, according to the account, "Some objections were raised and the project was abandoned."

Also in 1883, with the arrival of Henry Wagbo, soon to be followed by Andrew Berg and Anton Waldstad,

This 1884 Memorial Day gathering in downtown East Jordan brought together many Civil War veterans. The banner on the left identifies the Stevens Post, No. 66, of the GAR (Grand Army of the Republic). It was an influx of Civil War veterans that provided many of the East Jordan area's first homesteaders. *Photo from the collection of Virginia Kaake-Giacomelli.*

the homesteading of the Norwegian settlement south of town began.

During this same time there were distant rumblings of county seat troubles. Boyne City, thinking Charlevoix was too far off in a corner of the county, began agitating removal of the county seat to their town. It needed 11 of the 16 votes to secure it but only 10 could be mustered. Finally, at the October 1884 session, 11 supervisors designated East Jordan for the county seat and in the 1885 spring election the motion carried.

However, in the October 1885 session Boyne City secured the necessary two-thirds vote to move it from East Jordan to Boyne City. While the removal from Charlevoix to East Jordan was a quiet affair, the move to Boyne was another matter. Much illegal voting was charged. Both attracted a large vote, with probably as much illegality on one side as the other. East Jordan claimed that Boyne held back its vote until enough of the county had been heard from to show they had lost. Then 150 votes were placed in the ballot box and the returns announced accordingly.

Whether true or not, it caused bitter feelings through the entire county. A majority of the board of supervisors favored Boyne as the county seat. Judge Ramsdell also recognized Boyne as the county seat. County Clerk S. B. Thatcher and Sheriff Captain Berdan moved their offices to Boyne. Register of Deeds Fred J. Meech and Treasurer Orlando Blair refused to move. One or two ineffectual attempts were

made to steal the records and remove them by force.

The State Board of Equalization met that year (1886) so it was necessary that the Board of Supervisors get together in August to equalize the rolls but they couldn't agree on a meeting place. The result was that part of them met in each town. Not much business was accomplished by the groups in either Boyne or East Jordan, but to avoid trouble with the state board, the rolls were left unassessed.

Boyne Falls, thinking they might get the county seat on a compromise, threw in with East Jordan but it again lost. East Jordan next tried Bay Springs in Bay Township and the Register of Deeds and County Treasurer moved their offices there. At the October, 1886 session eight supervisors met at each place, Bay Springs and Boyne City. They were only a mile apart but it was still a deadlock.

Finally, Oscar Upright, a Charlevoix supervisor, voted for Boyne City, which ended the fight. It was not until the January 1897 meeting that Charlevoix, after an involved procedure, succeeded in getting the county seat back.

However, in 1886, East Jordan wasn't entirely preoccupied by the county seat controversy. George B. Martin organized the first East Jordan bank that year. He opened in the D. C. Loveday store until his frame building on the northeast corner of Esterly and Main was com-

TOP: In this 1910 photo, a crew stands around the smelter of the East Jordan Iron & Chemical Company, one of the community's largest industries at the time. *Photo from the collection of George Secord.*

BOTTOM: Market hunting for deer was allowed in the early part of the century; this shipment from East Jordan is shown being readied in 1915. *Photo from the collection of Connie Baker.*

pleted. In 1891, he sold the bank to Alexander Bush and Reuben R. Glenn, who operated it under the name of Bush & Glenn. Reuben died in 1895 and Bush sold his interest to Reuben's father, Joseph C. and his brother, George G. Glenn in 1897. In 1899, the Glenns replaced the frame structure with a brick building. In July, 1901 it was reorganized as a State Bank, with a capitalization of $20,000 and Joseph C. Glenn as president, Walter L. French as vice president, and George G. Glenn as cashier.

The Methodist church was organized and construction began on their church building on May 20, 1886. A third project that year was the erecting of the South Arm Township Hall at the intersection of Mill, State and Third Streets. Besides the town and township offices, it housed a jail on the first floor and a large meeting room on the third floor where the high school also played basketball games in the early 1900s.

According to Mattie Palmiter, one time the Methodists and Presbyterians held a series of union meetings there and, when they concluded, the Presbyterians walked off with all of the song books.

The Loveday family arrived in East Jordan in 1886. Douglas C. and his son W. Asa, bought the Jerrue building, converting it into a hardware store, with their living quarters above. They were to impact East Jordan's commercial and civic life for many years.

Another family who would be prominent in the city's future came the following year when Robert Mackey started a livery business. Later his son Rosco continued the business and eventually obtained a Ford auto dealership known as the Northern Auto Company. He and Asa Loveday helped establish the first East Jordan Board of Trade for which the articles of incorporation were filed in October 1903. Mackey and Rollin Bisbee also formed the Northern Finance Company.

Early in 1887, East Jordan was granted a charter as a village. The first meeting of the village council was held in April and called to order by village president J. H. Bennett. The following trustees were sworn in for one year: George W. Fust, John C. Jordan, and A. P. Porter; for two years: Isaac W. Bartlett, George B. Martin, and Joseph E. Potter.

This was also the year of the "big fight" at the Commercial House. The date: March, 1887. The East Jordan area was full of lumberjacks as many mills were operating in the vicinity. Of all the rough and tumble lumberjacks, the Ferguson brothers took the cake. There were seven of them: Alex, Bob, Dunc, George, Jim, John, and Bill. As Ernie Barnes said,

"I wouldn't say they learned fighting at their mother's knee, but they go no farther than the doorstep." G. A. Lisk, in his Charlevoix County Herald put it a little more bluntly, "When they and their cronies got together they could raise enough hell to keep three towns lively."

My account of the fight came from four eye witnesses: John Kenny, Asa Loveday (the club Asa carried that night still hangs in the Loveday house), Jake Strong, and John Whiteford. Lillian Brabant told of listening to the yelling while standing in her yard in South Arm.

The show got on the road when Town Marshall Robert McMillan went to the barroom of the Commercial House to arrest someone. The men didn't let him in as there was probably a question in their minds as to who he was after. The fight started just outside on the "sample room" lawn. Involved were Alex, Bill, Dunc and George Ferguson, Bill and Jack Muckle, Solon Barnes, Bill Dunlap, and Albert Kile. Bill Dunlap, Sr. was accused of being in it, but he hadn't arrived in time.

McMillan hit two or three men with a cant hook handle then went out and tried to arrest Alex Ferguson who was singing in the middle of the street, but Alex knocked him down. Dr. Judson Bennett, president of the village council, was fighting with one of the Muckles. Dan Caton, who had a meat market behind the bank, came out with his meat cleaver but didn't use it. The fighting continued until they reached the Loveday hardware, then they broke and headed for the bridge and South Arm with a number of the townspeople in pursuit.

Jake and Asa also told me of the time there was a rumor that Boyne City was going to come over that night and try and steal the court house. All the lumberjacks were in town so they could be in on the fun. About 11 p.m. things had quieted down (too quiet to suit the 'jacks), so Dunc Ferguson and Jack Muckle went on a window breaking spree up Main Street. The "fun" culminated in them picking up night marshall Jesse Weikel and throwing him through a window when he attempted to arrest them. They then went to Stambough for a few months until things quieted down.

Years later, when they got too old to fight, Bob Ferguson became a preacher and Jack Muckle became a conservation officer. I had a visit with Bob when he was back in East Jordan for a few days in 1938. He allowed that the town was "sure pretty quiet."

The last item we find regarding the Ferguson boys

TOP: Lillian and Charles Brabant are shown in their downtown East Jordan clothing store in this undated photo. *Photo from the collection of George Secord.*
BOTTOM: Blacksmith Charles T. Dickinson is shown working on horseshoes in this 1912 photo of an East Jordan Lumber Co. camp blacksmith shop. This was an essential part of each camp, since the only means of skidding logs out of the woods was teams of horses. *Photo from the collection of George Secord.*

appeared in the Charlevoix County Herald on June 6, 1902. Alex and Dunc picked a fight with Charles Henderson. The Herald continues, "Mr. Henderson defended himself as best he could until the arrival of village Marshall Johnson, who took charge of the Fergusons and with some assistance took them to jail, finding it necessary to club them into submission. When it was all over Alex looked as if he had been run through a thrashing machine while his brother fared little better. Tuesday morning they were brought separately before Justice Clement and both entered pleas of guilty. They were sentenced to 90 days at hard labor in the Detroit House of Correction."

In 1891 W. Harvey Porter, a distant relative of W. P. Porter, built a dam on Deer Creek and erected a water powered grist mill. The following year D. C. Loveday and son, Asa, built East Jordan's first electric plant at the foot of Williams Street. In October, 1902 Loveday

bought the grist mill and enlarged the dam to produce more power, using a steam plant as an auxiliary source of electricity. He also planned to use part of the new power plant to run the grist mill and eventually move the steam plant to the Deer Creek site. However, the wheels of the East Jordan Roller Mills turned for the last time April 15, 1903.

1892 was an eventful year for the young town. South Arm moved the original school and replaced it with a fine two-story, four room frame school on the same land. The entire community continued to grow as more industry arrived and general farming increased in the surrounding area.

The harbor was filled with freight and lumber schooners. W. E. Malpass once told me he had seen as many as 18 ships loading at the same time at the East Jordan and South Arm docks. There were also numerous small passenger boats plying between East Jordan

East Jordan's old Central School was built in 1893. The bell went on to be used in the Lutheran Church. *Photo from the collection of George Secord.*

and Charlevoix where the Chicago & West Michigan Railway had arrived in 1891. Another noteworthy item was the destruction by fire of the Commercial House in October.

But by far the major newsworthy event of the year was the destruction of the East Jordan Lumber Company's Mill "B," the "Big Red Mill," by a boiler explosion at 7:25 a.m. on March 21. The explosion killed seven people instantly and injured several more, including one who would die two weeks later. Those killed were Willie Beach, 16; John Brown, 23; Simon Carney, 26; Amzi Christie, 36; Albert Cook, 28; Emanuel Hunt, 40; and Peter Sheldon, 25. Hunt and Sheldon had gone to the mill that morning to seek employment. Sanderson Reinhart died later.

The mill was rebuilt and continued to run until it was destroyed by fire in March, 1914. Rebuilt once more, it ran until lumbering came to an end in 1928. The Red Mill sat idle until Sunday, August 4, 1935. Monday morning's Grand Rapids Herald, in front page headlines, told the story: "Ancient Landmark, the Red Mill is gone." It went on to say, "Standing on the shore of Pine Lake (now Lake Charlevoix), an ancient landmark, which lived a colorful tempestuous history, Sunday afternoon made the headlines for its third and final time. At 2:00 p.m. on a hot, humid afternoon, fire struck and, an hour later, the Red Mill was just a memory. A strong northwest

At the corner now occupied by the East Jordan City Hall, local residents gathered in December, 1915 to light the community Christmas Tree. Just to the right in the photo is the Empey Furniture Store which was later an A&P grocery market. *Photo from the collection of Virginia Kaake-Giacomelli.*

wind carried burning embers across the city, setting numerous roof fires and gutting two buildings. So give the gallant old girl full credit. If she had to die, she would go down fighting and take as much of the town as she could with her."

In 1893 East Jordan, not to be outdone by South Arm, built the first brick school on the site of the present middle school.

A second newspaper made its appearance in 1896. Harrison Mitchell started publishing the Charlevoix County Herald. It must have been a "hot potato" to handle, as everyone kept dropping it. Mitchell sold it to Andrew Suffern the following year. Suffern sold to Moritz Thimmig in 1900 and he turned it over to Roy Lorraine in 1901. George A. Lisk bought from Lorraine in 1904 and it remained in the Lisk family until 1953. G. A. retired in 1952 and his son, Paul, took over. Paul sold to Mr. and Mrs. Marshall Sayles in 1953 and the name was changed to the East Jordan News-Herald.

The last three years of the century brought many changes to the area. In 1897 Alexander Bush was buying right-of-way for David Ward's Frederic & Charlevoix Railway, to extend it from Alba to South Arm. Ward died on May 29, 1900, but his estate completed the line. By 1901 the railroad was fully installed and the Ward estate mill at Deward about ready to begin operations. On January 4,

Built in 1880 as the Chattuck House hotel on a site later to be occupied by the Hite Drug Store, this downtown landmark was renamed the Commercial House. It was the site of the infamous "Big Fight of 1887." *Photo from the Portside Art and Historical Museum collection.*

1901, the railroad was officially incorporated and its name changed to Detroit & Charlevoix. Regular passenger service began between Frederic and South Arm by the end of the year.

The D&C built a 500 foot transfer dock into Pine Lake, a mile north of South Arm, where trainloads of lumber from the Deward mill were transferred directly from flat cars to Great Lakes lumber ships. The Deward mill closed in March, 1912, and in 1916 the D&C was deeded to become the East Jordan branch of the Michigan Central Railroad. East Jordan was abandoned as a station of the Michigan Central in 1931. The last train between Frederic and East Jordan ran on June 30, 1931, manned by Conductor David Montour, Engineer P. T. Hendrie, with engine #8284, a 4-6-0 ten-wheeler. The tracks were taken up in 1932.

At the same time, Bush was buying right-of-way for the D&C, the East Jordan Lumber Company was building grades for a railroad into their Antrim County timber holdings. In November, 1898, the steam barge "Pine Lake" under Captain "Roaring Jake" Small delivered the first locomotive. It was obtained from Chicago's Lake Street elevated and would become East Jordan & Southern #1. John Porter told seeing it unloaded and his bitter disappointment at first sight of it. He thought his father had been taken because it didn't even have a cowcatcher.

In 1900 South Arm Township raised $15,000 to have the railroad completed into Bellaire to connect with the Pere Marquette. It became a common carrier in 1901, handling mail, passengers and freight. So, as 1902 dawned, East Jordan had direct connections with three of the state's four north and south trunk railroads, the Grand Rapids & Indiana at Alba, the Michigan Central at Frederic, and the Pere Marquette at Bellaire. Only the Detroit & Mackinac eluded us.

By now, Asa Love-day believed East Jordan was ready for a dose of culture so his father bought the Will Stone roller rink on the corner of Main and Williams where the G. A. R. Park is now and converted it into the Loveday Opera House. It opened in August, 1899 with Fred Conrad presenting "A Wise Woman."

However, East Jordan had an earlier "opera house" of sorts, not so well known as the Loveday. This was located in Joseph Maddock's barn. The stage was the haymow and the admission was three pins for older kids, two pins for wee ones. Many a mother went frantic when, starting to make a dress she found that most of her pins had disappeared. Lill Weikel Ramsey once told me, "If you think our mothers were mad, you should have heard Mr. Maddock when he would walk on hot evenings, around the barn barefoot. You could have heard him clear to Chestonia."

The local "stock" company wrote their own scripts and designed their own scenery. All performances were of the "burnt-cork Minstrel" (black-face) type. How their mothers scolded them as they tried to scrub it off. The youngsters sat, open mouthed, on the barn floor as

they watched the star performances of such actresses as Isabel Alexander, Lizzie and Sadie Mackey, Becky and Emma-Lill Weikel, Hattie Tencate, and Rachel Trimble, with Eddie Alexander as manager.

The Loveday Opera House always presented top-drawer stage and musical attractions, and the D&C ran many excursions to the shows from Dewardand Alba. Unfortunately, as so often happened in those days, a fire caught up with it and it was totally destroyed in the spring of 1910.

In April, 1899 the village voted to install a waterworks system and the project was completed that summer. The tower consisted of a timber supported, wooden tank sitting on top a 30-foot brick base. It stood just north of Garfield, between Third and Fourth Streets. By 1908 some of the supporting timbers were showing signs of decay so and it was decided to build a storage tank on the hill north of Division Street. Work progressed on the new facility but before it was finished the old tank got tired of waiting and started to lean towards the west. On Sunday, June 7 at 2 p.m. that section of East Jordan got the fastest, most lavish, combination tub and shower bath in the history of Northern Michigan and, best of all, it was free.

The force of the water hurled sections of the three foot thick brick walls some 30 feet away. An emergency steam pump, loaned by the East Jordan

---

BULLETIN
Charlevoix County Herald
Monday, Sept. 27th, 1920

Charlevoix Co. Census

Below figures were received Monday from the Bureau of Census, Washington. It shows a falling off in population of the County of 3369 from the 1910 figures. Only one township—Marion—shows an increase. Decreases in the three cities are—Boyne City 934, Charlevoix 202, and East Jordan 88.

Years	1920	1910	1900
Charlevoix County	15788	19157	13956
CITIES			
Boyne City	4284	5218	912
Charlevoix	2218	2420	2079
East Jordan	2428	2516	1205
TOWNSHIPS			
Bay Township	378	466	503
Boyne Valley Twp., including Boyne Falls village	807	952	1258
Chandler Township	259	397	273
Charlevoix Township	101	207	178
Evangeline Township	226	228	342
Eveline Township	594	768	847
Hayes Township	708	854	780
Hudson Township	209	673	255
Marion Township	694	636	681
Melrose Township	466	675	620
Norwood Township	292	366	652
Peaine Township	243	370	372
St. James Township	536	695	420
South Arm Township	744	910	1634
Wilson Township	601	806	945

The decline of the Lumber Boom in the East Jordan area is evident in these census figures charting the 1900-1920 period. Between 1900 and 1910 the population of East Jordan more than doubled, but the growth of Boyne City was even more astounding. *From the William Huckle collection.*

Collapse of Water Tower June 7, 08 E Jordan.

TOP: East Jordan's first water tower, a wooden storage tank supported by a 30-foot brick base, was located just north of Garfield Street between Third and Fourth Streets. It collapsed on June 7, 1908, sending a deluge of water and debris throughout the neighborhood. Luckily the city had previously noticed deterioration in the tower's supporting timbers and was already working on a new water tower when the old one collapsed. *Photo from the collection of George Secord.*

RIGHT: A fixture on the East Jordan waterfront for many years was the Argo Milling Co. *Photo from the collection of William Huckle.*

Lumber Company and supplied with steam from the East Jordan Electric Light Company, was coupled up that afternoon and water mains were kept operating by direct pressure until the new supply tank on Water Tower Hill was brought into service.

Another project of 1903 was the construction of a brick village hall, with a fire hall on the first floor. It was completed late that summer (and ultimately burned in 1948).

East Jordan and South Arm were finally incorporated into one village in 1905 with one Post Office on the east side. The business districts on both sides of the lake seemed to flourish during the next few years. C. A. Bayliss opened his East Jordan Brickyard in August, 1907. Two years later Harry Price, who built many of the town's homes and commercial buildings, also began manufacturing brick.

On December 16, 1907 the East Jordan Electric Light & Power Company had a headache on their hands. Early that morning a portion of the Deer Creek dam gave way releasing a 28-foot head of water which swept into the Jordan River and on down to Pine Lake. The new Deer Creek bridge, built by Charles Crowell a few years earlier, held solid. But when the wall of water hit the Jordan, it developed a counter-current which lifted the Monroe (now Rogers) bridge off its foundation and carried it eight rods upstream.

The water filled the flat lands, wrecking the East Jordan & Southern's bridge over the creek, and also washed out a section of the Detroit & Charlevoix's track near the lower stretch of the river. The D&C track was repaired sufficiently to allow trains to pass the next afternoon. The EJ&S also had to use the D&C tracks until a temporary bridge could be constructed over Deer Creek. No repairing could be done on the dam until the next spring. Over the winter the auxiliary steam plant in town was able to furnish enough power to meet everyone's needs.

At the peak of East Jordan's days as a timber loading port, schooners called "lumber hookers" would crowd the harbor. East Jordan Iron Works founder W.E. Malpass, who serviced many of these vessels with boiler grate and other repairs, recalled seeing as many as 18 vessels in and around the docks at one time. *Photo from the collection of William Huckle.*

The communities of South Arm and East Jordan were originally two separate villages connected by this bridge, which had a swinging span to allow vessel access to docks on the mouth of the Jordan River. The sign atop the bridge threatens a $10 fine for driving horse teams across the bridge faster than a walk. *Photo from the collection of William Huckle.*

April 2, 1910 saw the town lose a business but also gain one. Early that morning the Loveday Opera House was gutted by fire. That very afternoon, C.J. Bisbee and his son, Rollin and M. A. Honeywell arrived in East Jordan from Bad Axe, Michigan, bought the Miles building on Main Street and started plans to convert it into the town's second bank. Remodeling got under way in June and the People's State Savings Bank opened in the fall. Among local investors were Rosco Mackey, John Porter and William A. Stroebel.

Soon after the loss of the Loveday House, there began a feeling in town that they needed another amusement place so Harry Price, always civic minded and energetic, organized a small poker party one

evening. Before it was over the East Jordan Realty Company was born with Walter French, president; Earle Crossman, vice president; Wm. C. Spring, secretary; and George Glenn, treasurer. These four, with Price, William Stroebel and Burton E. Waterman comprised the board of directors.

B. H. Christian of Ludington was hired to design the building which contained a theater (main floor and balcony) seating 800, two stores in front, and a large ballroom above. Construction started the next spring and the Temple Theatre had its grand opening on October 17, 1911. It opened with a New York road company presenting "Madame Sherry," a French musical comedy with a cast of 19 people, including Franklyn Farnum playing the

Main Street, East Jordan, Mich.

By 1919 when this photo of downtown East Jordan was taken, horse drawn wagons and buggies were beginning to share the streets with automobiles, and the community was on the verge of many changes. *Photo from the collection of William Huckle.*

lead and Tessa Costa in the role of Yvonne. She would soon be one of the country's top musical stars. Farnum was already at the top.

About this time a group of theatrical people were buying property on the southeast edge of East Jordan and building homes in which to spend their off-seasons. They called the colony "Cherryvale." They generally arrived in May and hit the road again in mid-September to start rehearsal for the coming season.

Among those who built, and their stage names, were the Ellis Hartmans, a dancing team (Hartmand & Varady); the John Carlisles (Hanson & Drew); the John Phillips (Phillips & Bergen); the Jules Walters (Walters & Llewellyn); the Frank Grubers (Gruber & Kew); and Al Warda.

Some returned to East Jordan after retiring from the stage to spend the remainder of their lives here, often taking active roles in the civic and social life of the town. The last member of the Cherryvale group was Louise Walters Johnson (Louise Llewellyn) who died in 1943.

On July 1, 1911, East Jordan was incorporated as a city, and that brings to a close the pioneer era of the city. Although many people in the community probably didn't realize it at the time, the automobile and airplane were already beginning to shape the future. 🌱

William Fletcher Empey and the naming of East Jordan

BY TERRY GRAHAM

Born in 1840 near Kingston, Ontario, William Fletcher Empey was to be a very important person in the settlement of what today is East Jordan.

His family immigrated from Ireland and located near the village of Lanark in Ontario. William Empey immigrated to Michigan from Canada, most likely through the port of Detroit. Before settling permanently in northern Michigan, he worked for a Toledo-based company locating pine land for timber.

William Empey registered to vote in South Arm in 1873, a year prior to his moving to the area, and became a permanent resident in 1874. He built a general store in South Arm that was reputed to be the first building in the area with a shingled roof. After residing in the area for a few years, Empey attained the position of Commissioner of Highways in South Arm which meant that he was also responsible for keeping track of all registered voters and persons living in the area. In addition, he held the position of moderator in the Mayhew School District in 1877.

But Empey's most important contribution to the area is that he was the person who named East Jordan.

This process was somewhat tedious and very time consuming. First, a name was submitted to the Federal Post Office in Washington so they could check their records to see if any place else in the state held that name. If not, the applying community could use its chosen name.

Empey repeated this process about six times as his submitted names kept being rejected. He finally sent a list of names to the Post Office and had them pick one that was not in use. The Post Office selected "East Jordan" and appointed William Empey as the community's first Postmaster.

The first East Jordan Post Office was located in Empey's General Store. The building, a two story structure typical of the later 1800s, also housed the Enterprise (the local newspaper) and Odd Fellows Hall on the second level. In November of 1883, the store and everything in it was destroyed by fire. While rebuilding, he kept active by handling wood and bark and also engaged in farming.

According to the census of 1880, Empey was listed as a "huckster" or, vegetable seller, and was popularly known as "Fletch" to the villagers. His wife Ellen sold millinery goods (hats and clothing) in the General Store. Empey had a stepson named Frank Brotherton. It was believed that Brotherton was the brother of Ellen and moved to East Jordan with Mr. and Mrs. Empey.

The Empey's belonged to many social organizations of the day such as the Jordan River Lodge No. 159 and the I.O.G.T. (International Organization of Good Templars) in which each held some sort of official position. Empey also belonged to the North Star Tent, No. 130 and was a charter member of the Jordan River Lodge, F & A.M. (Free and Accepted Masons).

He continued in business until around 1900, at which time he went to Canada for a few years, returning in 1904 with his brother Joseph. Two years later William and his brother purchased the stock of furniture from J. J. Vortruba and opened Empey Brothers Furniture.

In 1909, Empey remarried, this time to Harriet Smith, who would eventually become the librarian. His stepson, Frank, was the auditor for the East Jordan and Southern Railroad Co. On April 5, 1913 disaster struck the Empey Brothers Furniture Company. The business was destroyed by fire and nothing survived.

In October of 1920, after living a long and very fulfilling life, William Fletcher Empey, one of East Jordan's earliest settlers, passed away at his home located on State Street. His cause of death is listed as a complication of diseases coupled with old age. 🍂

TOP: East Jordan had a community band for many years around the turn of century. From this photo it appears they sometimes had as much fun dressing up for concerts as playing in them. From left are Jack Barlett, Matt Swofford, Ellis Malpass, Fred Whittington, Leo Martinek (holding the banner), Gus Muma, Joe Weisman, Frank Martinek and John Green. *Photo from the Portside Art and Historical Museum collection.*

BOTTOM: With different trains using the same tracks in the early days, there was bound to be the occasional meeting . This collision on August 16, 1910 involved the East Jordan & Southern Railroad. *Photo from the collection of Virginia Kaake-Giacomelli.*

Lumber camp life

BY BILL PORTER

Handling logs at the camp required specialized equipment. Shown above on the left is the horse-drawn katydid used to haul logs from the woods to the rail spur. There a steam loader, the machine above with the large boom, would load them onto rail cars. *Photo from the collection of Virginia Kaake-Giacomelli.*

I was born in 1915 and remember going out to the lumber camps as a young boy. The camps were named according to the section on which they were built. So Camp Nine was built on Section Nine of Jordan Township, Camp 23 on Section 23, and so on. The East Jordan Lumber Company operated close to 100 different camps over the years it was in business, but ran only two or three camps at any one time.

The typical lumber camp would have 60 to 80 men working in it. Most would live during the week in large shanties provided by the camp and eat their meals in the cook shanty. Some would build shacks out in the woods and have a wife and a couple of kids there so

they could eat at home instead of with the lumberjacks all the time.

It was tough to beat the cooking at the camp, however. It was good food, very rich, and the men got all they could eat. As kids we would go out there on the train on Saturday mornings and arrive after the lumberjacks had left for the woods. The camp cook always had plenty of hot coffee, doughnuts, cake and other good things out for snacks. For the noon meal he would cut big three-inch chunks of beef, place them on flat cake pans and put them into the ovens.

They also ate a lot of potatoes. Once, when I went out to a camp with my dad, we happened to walk by one of the chore boys peeling potatoes. The boy would take a potato, most of which weren't too big to start with, and slice off thick pieces until he was left with something not much bigger than a french fry. Dad said, "Now look here. You take a potato that big and cut a slab like that, you've got no potato left!" It embarrassed me to have my dad get after him like that, but it was true; the boy was peeling two bushels of potatoes to get one to cook.

The camp cooks would fix rich desserts like raisin pies and we'd bring out big cookies baked by my Aunt Hamilton who was a well known cook in Grand Rapids' best restaurants before she retired and came north. These were five-inch diameter cookies made with lots of butter and sugar. They are still a favorite in our family even today.

You couldn't eat too much of that stuff unless you were doing a lot of hard work like the lumberjacks. And they couldn't do the work without all those calories. Imagine swinging an axe or sawing on a log ten hours a day. It was very, very hard work.

Most of the logging was done during the winter when logs could be transported by sled on the snow and frozen ground. On a cold day a lumberjack would wear one or two sets of long underwear, wool pants, wool shirt, wool jacket and leather mittens with wool mittens under-

neath. They would also wear overalls with the legs "docked," or cut off right below the knees so they wouldn't get wet and frozen from the snow. Some wouldn't change their long underwear for days or weeks at a time. They may have smelled bad, but everyone else did too, so I guess it didn't matter to them.

The logs would be piled on two sets of sleigh runners. The loads were usually as high as the sleigh was wide and very heavy; about 20 to 25 tons. You can see some pictures of logs piled very, very high but these were just done for show. These loads were always hauled downhill, never uphill, either to a railroad spur for loading or to the river where they could be floated to the mill. Hardwood logs to be floated would have to be tied onto some cedar logs or something, otherwise they would sink. Many that did sink are probably still on the bottom of the Jordan River or Lake Charlevoix.

The East Jordan & Southern Railroad was originally built to haul logs. After somebody would start cutting on a section of land way out in the woods they'd run the railroad out to it and they'd cut all the logs, load them on and haul them down here to the mill.

To move logs and lumber around the property, the lumber company had 40 or 50 big horses. Pierce Wiesler was a super

TOP: Early lumberjacks in East Jordan relied on the cross cut saw as their primary tool for felling trees such as this white cedar. *Photo from the Portside Art and Historical Museum collection.*

BOTTOM: Many old logging camp photos such as this show proud 'jacks posing atop huge piles of logs. To the relief of the horses, most of these were taken just for show; sleigh loads were usually no higher than the width of the sleigh. *Photo from the collection of Virginia Kaake-Giacomelli.*

A horn blast or two from the chore boys would bring the lumber jacks in for a hearty noon meal. *Photo from the Portside Art and Historical Museum collection.*

six o'clock in the morning and go down to the chemical works to get all the flat cars that were empty. It would bring them down by the Argo Mill and then up to the big mill to get all the rustle cars. Then we'd go down by the roundhouse and the guys from the company store would have a big sleigh load of supplies that they needed at the camp. We'd load that into the caboose and go.

The engine would haul about 20 flat cars, then the caboose, then about 100 rustle cars. We'd have the caboose all fired up so it was warm for the guys to ride in. A broom was always stuck upright on the last car and as long as we could see the broom we knew that we had the whole train with us. If we lost the broom, we'd have to back all the way up to where the cars had come unattached.

They built the first railroad out of town in about 1898 and that was just for logs. When they got as far as Hitchcock

teamster. He understood horses and would go down there at 5 a.m. to brush the horses, feed them grain and get them all ready to go to work. Then he'd go home for breakfast and come back down at 7 o'clock, harness the horses up and go to work.

On Saturday mornings, I would get Bill Malpass and a couple other kids together to ride the train out to the camps. We'd get the fire going in the caboose stove while the train crew went about assembling log cars and cordwood cars. The engine would start out about

they decided it might as well hook up with the Pere Marquette. Then the railroad was expanded to have passenger service, mail and express. That kept the railroad going for a long time because there was no other way to get here. You couldn't haul mail with a wagon from Grand Rapids and going by boat was too slow.

By 1928, the lumber camps were pretty much all done. But they were a very important part of East Jordan's history.

TOP: This photograph of a typical East Jordan area lumber camp at the turn of the century shows the cluster of buildings in which the crews would live during the winter season. Also evident is the logging activity that had occurred around the camp. *Photo from the Portside Art and Historical Museum collection.*

BOTTOM: Good food, and plenty of it, was one of the perks of early lumber camps. Here the men are shown at a typical mid-day spread. *Photo from the collection of George Secord.*

The Stanek Family

BY VIRGINIA STANEK REED

My grandparents all came to the East Jordan area from the old country. My father's parents, the Staneks, both came from Moravia. My mother's father, David Shepard came from England at the age of four and her mother, Anna Votruba immigrated from Prague, Czechoslovakia when she was 13.

Grandma (Svoboda) Stanek sailed at age 11 with her family from Bremen, Germany in 1868. After a voyage of 12 days they landed in New York and from there went to Detroit, just a village at the time. Then it was on to Racine, Wisconsin for two years and then to the Pine River at Charlevoix. They carried provisions to Jordan Township and built log huts covered with elm bark.

Grandma Shepard often told stories of how her family came by boat to what is now Rogers Bridge on the Jordan River. The women and girls carried bed quilts, pillows and ticks made of stripped feathers. All farm and food supplies were carried on their backs from the river to farmsteads where log homes were built. Oxen were used to farm the land.

Grandma's parents homesteaded on a piece of land next to what is now the St. John Nepomucene Catholic Church in the Bohemian settlement. Her oldest brother, Frank Votruba opened a harness store in Traverse City and her youngest brother, Jim Votruba ran a hardware store in East Jordan.

As a young lady, Grandma worked temporarily as a housemaid in Traverse City and the only means of transportation to Traverse City from her home was by foot. It took all of two days for her to make the walk so luckily there was a building of sorts near Eastport where she could spend the night. My father also recalled the two-day walks to Traverse City.

My father, who was born in 1883, could play the violin and would play on Saturday nights for entertainment. Dances were held at various farm homes where the rugs were rolled up and a pot luck supper shared. Barn dances were also regular events, especially when a new barn was built. Barns were always built with the volunteer labor of friends and neighbors.

My father took his violin almost everywhere he went. Once, however, he did not have it with him when he walked to a party being held about five miles north of the church, near where the Peninsula Grange now stands. When he arrived he learned that they had no music for dancing so he ran all the way back to get his violin. The music and dancing went all night and my father arrived home just in time to milk the cows and do all the morning chores. I myself remember the house dances, barn dances and Grange meetings.

I attended the one-room Brown School through eighth grade. Our school teacher usually roomed and boarded at my parents home. The number of students at the school ranged from six to 30 children at any given time. We had our own end-of-the-year picnics and Christmas programs in which all the children participated and exchanged presents. In the spring we would have our usual baseball games with all ages playing. One country school would play another; I think there were about six in the area that competed.

To get to town for supplies by wagon or sleigh, Dad would leave before daylight and get home after dark. We would be snowbound during most of the winter so he would make a trip at Christmas time, knowing that the next trip would likely be around Easter. During the winter we skied to school often, with some of the children coming from as far as three miles away.

On some winter Saturday nights we would set out with skis, sleds and toboggans for Fire Tower Hill, picking up more and more children as we passed farm homes. After a night of sliding we returned home the same way, dropping off each child at their own warm home.

A long, long trip to Thumb Lake

BY MARGUERITE STOKES

In 1869, newlyweds Samuel G. and Eleanor Rogers left Canada for a new life in Charlevoix County, Michigan. Samuel had visited the area with his father two years before and had picked out his homestead on Birney Creek bordering the Jordan River.

They cleared the land of trees and farmed, with their earliest crops being potatoes and turnips, two crops that could be grown between the stumps. These furnished valuable food for both man and beast and could be kept through the winter. Sam and Eleanor raised five children, the youngest of which, Sam E., married Maggie Ann Waggoner of Thumb Lake. Sam E. and Maggie had six children.

In those days, the only way Sam E. and Maggie could take their family to visit her parents in Thumb Lake was by horse and buggy. It was slow, but usually a leisurely and pleasant trip. The normal routine was to start out on Saturday afternoon and return on Monday. The buggy was a light, open one with no canopy so they were at the mercy of the elements.

The couple made one such trip to Thumb Lake when their first two children, Lem and Marguerite, were age five and one respectively. The family had gotten just past Boyne Falls when clouds appeared and a rain shower followed. The rain slowed their progress.

Maggie put up her big, black umbrella which she carried to provide their only protection against sun or rain. She held the umbrella with her right hand while cradling little Marguerite in her left arm. Lem had his own little chair from the house to sit on. A waterproof lap robe covered the children.

The horse, Prince, kept going but the conditions slowed their progress enough that darkness overtook them. It was such a deep, dark blackness that Sam could not even see to drive the horse and there were no houses at which to stop. Sam decided to let the horse have his head; that is, he let the reins go slack. Prince did not stop, but kept plodding steadily on. The children fell asleep under the robe.

After what seemed like an eternity, Prince stopped in his tracks. Sam clucked at him to go on but Prince only lifted a hoof and put it down. Maggie was a bit fearful as to why the horse had stopped. Sam carefully stepped down from the buggy and felt his way to the horse's head. He reached out his hand and discovered that Prince's nose was touching Grandpa Waggoner's gate.

Sam opened the gate and climbed back into the buggy. This time Prince continued on and shortly the faint light of the Waggoners' kerosene lamp came into view. Everyone was most relieved, including the Waggoners who had been worrying about the travelers.

This mode of travel continued until Sam bought his first Model T Ford. That meant no more buggy rides for the family, although Sam's parents continued to rely on a horse and buggy when they wished to go into town.

With the Model T, Sam E. could now go make the trip to Thumb Lake and back in a day, leaving early on a Sunday morning and returning the same evening. The kids always took along winter coats because it could get pretty chilly whizzing along at 15 to 20 miles per hour in an open vehicle after dark.

It was still quite a trip, chugging over roads which were poor by today's standards. Sometimes Maggie had to push the car up some sandy hills. She would lay the baby on the grass with the other children watching over her during the process. Sam tried to get his wife to drive so he could do the pushing but she did not take to driving a Model T.

In the 1920s Alfred and Sam Rogers formed Rogers Construction Co. which built many miles of concrete roads in Michigan.

The Rogers homestead on the Jordan River, established in 1869, has been occupied continuously by six generations of the family.

The Ironton Ferry

BY TOM BREAKEY SR.

The need for regular transportation across the South Arm at Ironton was evident for a long time before a ferry existed there. Around 1876 Robert Bedwin, who lived on the east approach, took people back and forth across the Ironton Narrows in a rowboat for five cents per trip.

The need for a more dependable crossing escalated with the opening of the new Iron Works. In addition, farmers on the peninsula needed a better means to get goods to market in Charlevoix.

In 1881, W. B. Stohman presented a petition to the Charlevoix County Board of Supervisors requesting construction of a ferry, but the request was not acted upon. The next petition was brought by 0. Miller on October 10, 1883, and on the next day the Board authorized Henry E. Sheldon, "to build and operate a ferry guided by a wire cable secured on each side (that) lies sufficiently deep in the water so as to offer no obstacle to navigation."

Tolls were set as follows:

Double teams	*30 cents*
Single teams	*20 cents*
Beasts	*10 cents except sheep*
Sheep	*10 cents up to six;*
	over six, 5 cents each
Footmen	*5 cents without beasts*
Threshing Machines	
and articles of such nature	*$1.00*

Three years later, the Board was petitioned to buy the ferry from Sheldon and run it as a free ferry with two-thirds of expenses paid by the County and one third paid by Eveline Township. Yearly costs were estimated at $225. A resolution was passed to buy the ferry for $150. The first county-hired ferryman,

The first cable-guided Ironton Ferry was authorized in 1883 and would transport a single team of horses across the South Arm for 20 cents. *Photo from the Portside Art and Historical Museum collection.*

BELIEVE IT OR NOT
By RIPLEY

While In Charlevoix County

Don't Fail to Cross the

SOUTH ARM

of Beautiful

Lake Charlevoix

With Capt. Sam Alexander

on the

IRONTON FERRY

Operated Free by Charlevoix County

SAM ALEXANDER FERRY BOAT OPERATOR HAS TRAVELED 15,000 MILES AND WAS NEVER FARTHER THAN 1000 FEET FROM HIS HOME!

And---

Made Famous by Ripley's "Believe It Or Not"

This advertisement for the Ironton Ferry capitalizes on the notoriety the ferry and Sam Alexander got from the popular "Ripley's Believe It or Not".

Robert Miller, Eveline Township clerk, was paid $1.25 per day.

The year 1899 saw the first gasoline engine installed on the ferry at a cost of $225. The four-horsepower engine pulled the ferry along the cable, a job that before had been strictly manual labor performed by the operator and passengers.

In 1910, Charlevoix County assumed full control of the ferry. Sam Alexander was hired to run the ferry for the years 1911 and 1912. Alexander was born in Quincy, Kentucky and came to Ironton in 1888. Upon his arrival he went to work at the Iron Works. In Ironton he met and married Harriett Williams, who was born and raised in Canada.

Hours of operation for the ferry were to be from 6:30 a.m. to 8:30 p.m. and Alexander was to be paid $65 per month, with a half hour off for dinner and twenty minutes off for supper. For this wage he was also expected to keep the scow and engine in good repair, furnish the necessary fuel and motor oil for operation, and in the spring cut a channel in the ice. The County furnished material for repair.

Early in Alexander's tenure, it was determined that the scow was in bad shape and needed replacing. The County agreed to furnish a new scow and engine, and allowed service to be extended to 24 hours per day.

Crossings from 6:00 a.m. to 8:30 p.m. were free, and service from 8:30 p.m. to 6:00 a.m. cost five cents for each foot passenger and a quarter for each vehicle. Alexander was allowed to keep all night-time tolls as pay for his work.

By 1926 a larger ferry was needed and a new Kahlenberg Diesel engine and scow was purchased for $23,765.00. This ferry proved to be a very good investment, since the engine was the ferry's sole source of power for more than 50 years. It was retired in 1978 due to the unavailability of repair parts. Old timers fondly remember how, as the ferry crossed on a windless day, it would leave a string of smoke rings from the engine exhaust.

Sam Alexander was contracted in two year increments to operate the ferry until he retired in 1942. By that time, he and the ferry had been made famous by Robert E. Ripley's "Believe It Or Not," column in newspapers coast to coast. The article stated that, in performing his job, Alexander had traveled 15,000 miles and was never farther than 1,000 feet from his home.

Tolls were reinstated in 1948 by which time operating costs had risen to nearly $8,000 per year. Fees set were: 15 cents for passenger cars and pickup trucks and 25 cents for commercial vehicles. Motorcycles, bicycles, and walkers rode free, unless a special trip was made.

The next year the Charlevoix County Board of Supervisors delegated ferry operation and maintenance to the County Road Commission. Rates and policies were set by the Supervisors and the Road Commission was reimbursed annually for actual expenses incurred. The ferry is now operated by the Charlevoix County Transportation Authority under a 1981 agreement. The county and the road commission share operating expenses equally.

The ferry has been repaired, rebuilt and replaced many times over the years; it bears little resemblance to that first little hand operated barge used in 1883. Now, because of it's designation as, "A Michigan Historical Site," the Ironton Ferry has been afforded permanent status. We can be assured it will be chugging back and forth across the South Arm narrows far into the future.

Fred Sweet and "The Good Old Times"

BY ROSE WESTCOTT

In February, 1878 a returning Union soldier from the 13th Michigan Volunteers named Sanford Sweet of Hastings, Michigan joined many of his comrades in seeking out a homestead in northern Michigan. Land had been made available to them free of charge by the government.

Sanford's search ended in Jordan Township of Antrim County. Since it was a fairly mild winter, Sweet decided to bring his wife and children up from Hastings right away and in early March they arrived by train in Boyne Falls.

The area between Boyne Falls and Chestonia was heavily wooded with virgin timber. Leaving his wife and two daughters with the Pinney family, Sanford and his two sons started out by foot on a woodland trail to the homestead. Near the site, they stopped at the home of a relative named Bert Brown to make arrangements for the rest of the family. A nearby family named Wilkes, who lived on the present Joe Chanda property, owned a pair of western ponies and consented to go for Mrs. Sweet and the girls.

However, Wilkes' wagon had no bed; only four wheels, two bunks and a reach. He went to Boyne Falls for lumber to build a bed in the wagon but could find only two pine boards for sale. These he laid across the bunks and upon them rode the rest of the Sweet family with all their boxes, trunks and other belongings. It was a ride to remember as in many places they had to get out and clear the road to get through.

After settling his wife and daughters at the Browns, Sanford and the boys started for the homestead. The youngest, Fred, was awed by the great trees and wilderness of it all. Arriving at the homestead, they started to build at once. Logs were cut, hewed to shape and hauled by horse and wagon into place. Fred carried along a chunk of wood to block the cargo at every stop.

Once the walls were up they started cutting poles for rafters and shakes for the roof. The two boards on the wagon came in handy again as they were cut and nailed to make a door. When it was finished, the fam-ily moved in and started the real labor of hewing a producing farm out of the unbroken land.

Fred grew up on that farm with his parents and brothers and sisters, watching as the surrounding country was gradually settled. He always enjoyed hunting and fishing in the wild areas the best, however, and became an expert in identifying productive game trails and fishing holes. He was a natural to become a guide for the local tourist trade.

A great deal of his guiding was done on the Jordan River which was widely known for its beauty and its fishing. People would start at the mouth of the river and travel several miles upstream on wide, flat-bot-tomed boats that were poled by hand. The Jordan flowed much faster then, with several small cataracts and a great deal of rough water. The river's banks were lined with bushes, ferns and overhanging trees and its waters abounded with speckled trout that, when fried over an open fire, had a flavor that a tourist from one of the southern counties would never forget.

A highlight of the journey upstream was the chan-nel leading to Graves Crossing which was very fast water and difficult to pole up. Some tourists would get out and walk the trail to make it easier but not all of them. Fred ended up with one particularly obese cou-ple, the Van Pelts, who not only kept their seats as he struggled to pole the boat up the channel, but fussed and wrangled for the entire journey. For this reason he refused to take them out the next day and was assigned instead to another group which, to his delight, turned out to be composed entirely of young ladies.

Fred liked best to take out the fishermen since they required little poling and wanted only a good spot in which to fish. One of his favorites was a druggist from Grand Rapids named Hazelton whom he dumped into the river once while bringing in a fish but who took it all in good sport and returned again and again.

At the age of 24 Fred met and married a girl from Alba. They lived in Alba for a while but then moved back to the farm where they built a new house and

The Jordan River, shown here at the original Munro Bridge, became widely known in the early 1900s for its quiet beauty and excellent fishing. *Photo from the collection of George Secord.*

his son Claude eventually be-came part of this booming industry.

After serving 12 years as a road commissioner for Antrim County and two as a state road com-missioner in East Jordan, Fred went into logging aggressively, running Camp 11 for the Porters and cutting off Sections 27 and 34.

Tragedy struck the family when 11-year old Ethel died in a fire at Fred's sister's home. Fred's wife had been in ill health and died not long after. Claude meanwhile married a girl named Velma White and their many children helped to ease Fred's loneliness. He continued to live alone, however in the home he built in 1891.

When I visited him there, he was 92 years old and had suffered two strokes. I certainly did not expect to find a chipper old gentleman with a house as neat as a pin, a sparkle in his eye and a mind that would do cred-it to someone many years younger, but that was the Fred Sweet I reminisced with that day.

The road to his house is quiet these days and the vacant homesites nearby look empty and forlorn to the passerby. But in Fred's mind they were alive with recollections of the "good old times" we always hear about, times we may not necessarily want to go back to, but which make for a wonderful treasure chest of memories.

raised two children, Claude and Ethel. These were the years of the loggers and lumber towns and Fred and

Remembering the Hum

BY ROBERT BOYCE

PASSENGER BOAT HUM EAST JORDAN, MICH

Making up to three round trips a day to Charlevoix, the steamer Hum, shown here at her dock in East Jordan, was a popular means of transportation in the early 1900s. *Photo from the Portside Art and Historical Museum collection.*

At the turn of the century, roads were poor and often snowbound, and horsepower came from real horses. Railroads were the preferred means of inner city travel. On the lakes, steam vessels carried passengers and package freight. Sail could compete only for bulk cargo such as lumber, iron ore and grain.

Perhaps because East Jordan and Charlevoix each had rail connections to the south and because they were only one and a half hours apart by steamer, they were never connected by rail.

Early in the century, three small streamers maintained seven round trips a day, carrying passengers and freight between East Jordan and Charlevoix.

Their catch phrase: "We stop on signal at all docks along the route." These boats were *Walter Chrysler, Jos. Gordon,* and *Hum.* Of these, *Hum* was the prettiest, the fastest and the last to operate on the Pine Lake (Lake Charlevoix) run.

Hum was built in 1876 as the steam yacht *Truant* for Truman H. Newberry of Detroit. She was 87 feet long, 16 feet wide, and powered by a 50-horsepower compound condensing steam engine. With her clipper bow, two tall masts, and lots of rigging (no sails) she was designed to resemble a sailing yacht.

The continuing good fortunes of Newberry prompted him to upgrade in 1892 to a bigger yacht which he also named *Truant.* In 1893 he sold the ear-

Before she was converted to a commercial steamer, Hum was a pleasure yacht known first as Truant, and then Pilgrim. *Photo from the Portside Art and Historical Museum collection.*

East Jordan and was converted from pleasure yacht to passenger/freight boat.

On September 12, 1903, the steamer, *Pilgrim* was involved in Lake Charlevoix's worst boating accident (see story on page 39). The next year, the vessel's name was changed to *Hum* .

George Jepson died in 1905. A rendering of *Hum* is engraved on his headstone in Charlevoix's Brookside Cemetery. *Hum* remained in the Jepson family and continued to operate on Lake Charlevoix until 1917.

In 1918, she was sold to John F. Miller of Chicago, rebuilt again as a passenger boat, and renamed *Howard F.*

From 1918 to 1934 *Howard F.* sailed on the Chicago waterfront between Municipal Pier and Lincoln Park. In 1935, at age 58, she was abandoned and sunk in the North Branch of the Chicago River, north of the Ashland Avenue Bridge.

lier *Truant* and she was renamed *Pilgrim*. By 1900 *Pilgrim* was on her sixth owner and was berthed in Charlevoix. She was sold that year to George Jepson of

The Stockade

BY JOAN SHERIDAN HOOVER

The conservative Norm Bartlett home on Kidder Road at M-66 was once a swinging beer garden called the Stockade Tavern. Everyone went there to drink, dance, and "shoot the bull." The establishment was advertised in huge letters across the roof: BEER and DANCE.

Originally 400 acres homesteaded by the Bennetts, the Bartlett family bought 80 acres of it in 1926 from the Federal Land Bank for $325. Norm and Jennie tore down the Bennett's two-story house and build a one story room to be used as the bar. The Stockade operated as a beer garden with "the world's best music" for only two years, 1939 and 1940. Norm recalls having, "about a dozen good customers and about 12 not so good."

Beer was popular at ten cents a glass, wine was 15 cents; hard liquor was not served. Favorite tunes were Beer Barrel Polka, South of the Border, Release Me, I'm Nobody Baby, Peg of My Heart, Five Foot Two, Baby Face, Bye-Bye Blackbird, Let Me Call You Sweetheart, and lots more. Norm remembers, "We had to put an extra post under the floor because when a crowd danced, the floor bounced."

The Second World War brought an end to all the fun. The booths were taken out, partitions were put back in and all the other amenities of a home added. It was never dull at the Bartlett house—what with three boys, how could it be?—but it never again matched the excitement of "Shooting the Bull at the Stockade!"

East Jordan's Bohemian Settlement

BY LUCY LERCEL

St. John Nepomucene was the setting for many baptisms, funerals and weddings, as shown here, within East Jordan's Bohemian community. *Photo from the Portside Art and Historical Museum collection.*

All we do is work, work, work and we still have nothing of our own. Let's go to America like our relatives. They also work hard but someday they will have their own land."

That was the feeling held by many natives of the Czechoslovakian province of Bohemia as they made the decision in the latter part of the 19th century to go to the "New Country." Most of the people who came to America from Czechoslovakia had worked for land owners in their home country. For their labor they were given a portion of the harvest, a portion that was typically harvested after the land owner's share, usually very late at night or in the rain.

Those who decided to leave left behind family, friends and a familiar way of life. They were prompted by letters from daring friends and relatives who had already immigrated to the United States. Advertisements by railroad companies in the newspapers also spurred them on.

James Svager and John Pesek were among the first of these immigrants to come to Antrim County. When they first arrived, they worked for the Antrim City lumber companies for very little pay. After eight years, Svager and Pesek decided to make a claim on some free land offered by the Homestead Act and carved a place out of the wilderness with no close neighbors.

The two families worked hard to make a shelter, clear the land and find food to live. Life was very hard for the pioneers but they were driven by the hope for a better life for their children.

As more of them came to the area, the Bohemian settlers would gather together and help each other. They built houses, barns and cleared the land for farming. Members of this close-knit neighborhood were there for each other in happy times as well as tragic times.

One thing many had in common was their Catholic faith. In the earliest days of the settlement there was no church so they would gather at one of the homes and James Svager would lead them in prayer and song. The budding congregation eventually wrote to Harbor Springs where a missionary was located and petitioned for a priest to come and say mass for them.

It was a day for rejoicing and celebration when a Catholic priest, Father Zorn, came to visit. Father Zorn advised them to build a school before a church, saying, "Church services can be held anywhere, but it is very important to educate the children."

A log school was built in 1877 on land donated by the Grand Rapids and Indiana Railroad Company. Frank Severance was the first teacher to educate the settlers' children in the new schoolhouse. The money from the sale of the land of every 16th section in the township was set aside for the school system. To encourage settling of the land, every even-numbered section was put up for homesteading by the federal government. All odd numbered sections were acquired by the railroads to encourage rail transportation.

The log school remained

until 1887 when a new frame school was built. The school operated until 1945 when it was consolidated with the East Jordan school system. The building still stands today at the corner of M-32 and St. John Road across from the stone church.

The Bohemian community continued to grow as more and more people came to the United States.

St. John Nepomucene Church was the focal point of the devoutly Catholic Bohemian Settlement. The church, completed in 1893, is shown, top, in its original state. A 1924 remodeling gave the church its distinctive fieldstone veneer, above, which it still has today. *Photos from the collection of Lucy Lercel.*

The homes soon became too small for the devoted Catholics to gather for weekly prayer and for mass when a priest visited. Even the Josifek's home, built with an extra large parlor specifically for that purpose, was too small. Thus it became necessary to build a church.

An acre of land was donated by John Votruba and in May of 1885 the pioneers happily began building their church. They were accustomed to working together but this was an exceptionally joyful task; the sound of native Bohemian songs rang out as they worked.

By the fall of 1885 they had a roof on the church and the structure was blessed by a Father Graf as St. John Nepomucene Catholic Church. St. John Nepomucene was a tenth century Bohemian cleric who was confessor to the queen of Czechoslovakia at the time. Enemies of the queen tried to force Nepomucene to renounce her but he refused and had his tongue torn out. Thus the statue of St. John Nepomucene that stands in the little stone church today is of the saint holding a finger to his lips.

John Votruba Jr., and Francis Swoboda were the first couple to be married in the church. Once the roof was on, however, progress slowed on the construction somewhat as parishioners worked on it whenever they could.

Mrs. Bertha Votruba gathered with her children for this family portrait, taken at one of East Jordan's first commercial photography studios, the Palmiter Studio. *Photo from the Portside Art and Historical Museum collection.*

The bell has been tolled for warnings of disasters and victory of war.

The Bohemian Settlement experienced its greatest development during the first decade of the twentieth century. The Settlement and St. John Nepomucene Catholic church were practically synonymous. In 1907 the church was enlarged, and sleeping quarters for visiting priests were added. The priests would come by rail to Boyne Falls, and one of the settlers would meet him there with horse and buggy for the last leg of the trip to St. John's.

Eventually the invention of the automobile and better roads made the sleeping quarters obsolete. In 1924, under the direction of Father Drinnan, the church was remodeled to its present form. A sanctuary, and a partial basement were added. Tom Jensen, a stonemason, was hired to add the fieldstone veneer. This unusual veneer is one of the reasons St. John Nepomucene Church was accepted to the Michigan Historical Commission in February 1993.

At the turn of the century there was a general store owned by John Votruba next to the church. This was also the location of a post office which was administrated by Frank Votruba, John's son, as the first postmaster. The store was closed in 1912 following the death of John Votruba.

The tiny church stood there, three windows to a side, no steeple, no bell, unfinished on the inside until 1893. With the encouragement of Fr. Bruno Torka, Francis Kolin erected a steeple and the bell was added. This bell, dedicated to St. Aloysius, is still there today.

Many of the structures of the Bohemian Settlement are no longer present, but the hard work and toil of these early pioneers can be felt in the landscape and in the caring family traditions that still survive among their descendants.

The Hite Drug Company

BY ANN HITE BISBEE

The Hite Drug Company was established in East Jordan in 1909 by Amos Jay Hite and his sister, Hannah Almina Hite (later to be known affectionately by everyone in town as "Aunt Mina"). The building they occupied stood where Vincent's Yamaha is currently located.

In 1911 they moved into the newly completed Boswell building at 209 Main Street. W.T. Boswell's photography studio and home was upstairs for many years. The Hites occupied the downstairs for 71 years. After purchasing the building from W.T. Boswell, the Hite family lived on Second Street in the summer and spent winters in the apartment over the store.

The store's original fixtures were purchased second-hand from Hazeltine and Perkins Drug Wholesalers in Grand Rapids in the early 1900s. Most of them are now back in what was the store, refinished and looking better than ever. The old tin ceiling is still in place, along with the wooden floors. The original ceiling fixtures are gone, but their light was inadequate at best. Many of the old pharmaceutical items can now be seen at the East Jordan Historical Museum at Elm Point.

For years the drug store was the only agent for the Railway Express Company and it also housed the only phone booth in town. After the phone booth was removed, a "candlestick" phone was installed nearer the front of the store and used by many townspeople. Incidentally, the telephone operators were located upstairs next door, working from a switchboard in the back room. The local newspaper was published and printed downstairs. The drug company also held the only Michigan Liquor Control Commission licenses for beer, wine, and liquor in East Jordan for over 50 years.

A. Jay Hite was a licensed pharmacist and Mina received her apprenticeship working for Dr. Warne, who also had a pharmacy in connection with his medical practice in East Jordan. She was his nurse, office help, Girl Friday, receptionist, buggy driver and also assisted at births and kitchen table operations. Obviously a woman far ahead of her time!

The Hite Drug Store as it looked in the early 1900s. *Photo courtesy of Ann Hite Bisbee.*

The brother and sister duo continued in business with young Jay assisting from the time he could reach the cash register and make change. It was a struggle to keep the store going during the Depression and also during World War II. After young Jay came home from the Air Force, it took another three years to complete his pharmacological education at what was then Ferris Institute. In the meantime, A. Jay died in 1949, before Jay finished college and Mina managed to keep the store open with the capable help of Bill Hawkins, and Jay commuting weekends from Big Rapids.

As for Aunt Mina, she worked every day in the store well into her 80s until she could no longer walk. Jay worked until stricken with a heart attack and was forced to sell the store in 1982. He always hoped he could work until at least 1986, making it the longest operating store in East Jordan owned by the same family—75 years!

The building is now enjoying a wonderful revival as the very successful Busy Bridge Antiques & Gifts. ✍

Cemeteries are windows to the past

BY LORNA PEEBLES

There are 15 cemeteries in the East Jordan area. If you are tracing your family tree or just want to spend an afternoon in reverence, a visit to one of these resting places can be a quiet, pleasant experience.

Within the city of East Jordan is Calvary Cemetery on Division Street and Sunset Hill on Sunset Street. Both cemeteries date back to the 1800s and both feature the large steeple-shaped stone memorials. These impressive memorials do not necessarily mark the places where people are buried, but rather stand in their memory.

The oldest identifiable grave marker in Calvary is that of Angeline and Francis Kenny who both died in 1893. The cemetery is dotted with white cement crosses but few have inscriptions that can be read. Of the tall steeple-shaped stones, some have different names on each of their four sides.

Sunset Hill has headstones dating back to the early 19th century, including one on the Gurner plot dated 1814. There are many simple, brick-sized stones with just the names "Baby," "Minnie" or "Franklin." Some of the older stones tell exactly when a person died: "83 years/1 month/10 days." Others identify who was responsible for placing the marker: "Erected by wife."

Whole families that may have suffered a great

These ornate memorials at the St. John Cemetery reflect the devout faith of East Jordan's Bohemian settlers and the richness of the Old World culture they brought to the area. *Photo by Karen Walker.*

tragedy are buried together. Some people who died at a young age are remembered by pictures on the stones. One is overwhelmed by sadness seeing these faces and the vitality they represent.

Venturing out of town in almost any direction, cemeteries can be found on many back roads. Jordan Township has the largest concentration of burial sites, probably because of the many different nationalities that settled there. The best remembered of these groups were the Bohemians who came to Jordan Township from Czechoslovakia and had their own church and cemeteries.

One definition of "Bohemian" is "one who lives unconventionally" and the St. John Nepomucene Pioneer Cemetery of 1871, located on Pesek Road, is definitely unconventional. Walking among the markers, one feels surrounded by love. Crosses dot the site which is dominated by a very large crucifix in the center. The crosses are made of stone, iron, pipe, wood and tin. Dates do not seem as important in this cemetery; just that the person is remembered. Names are etched, scratched and even written by marker. One very interesting cast iron grave marker is about six feet tall with a crucifix on top, a scull and cross bones under it and an angel holding a name plate inscribed in the person's native language.

As you are leaving this cemetery, be sure to look under the large pine tree there to find a marker for "Unknown Pioneer" hidden under the branches.

There are two other cemeteries within a mile either way from St. John's Nepomucene Church. On M-32 is Calvary Cemetery in which the oldest marker is that of Jerome B. Votruba who died in 1918. The site is surrounded mostly by cement family plots on the hillside. Down St. John's Road is the Jordan Township Cemetery in which the oldest marker is that of Karel Hejhal, dated 1909. Only five families are represented in this cemetery.

Brown Cemetery on the corner of Marsh and Stanek Roads is a small, neatly kept cemetery. Family plots are marked in four corners by stones with initials. The oldest identifies the daughter of A. & E. Brown, age 7 months, 7 days. There is also a beautiful small piece of marble marking one unnamed grave.

Rock Elm Cemetery on Morris Road is hidden in the woods. The oldest marker there is that of a P.A. Sleeper, dated 1880. Again, there are many stones marked only with initials.

Wilson Township has three cemeteries: Lewis on Healey road off Pleasant Valley, Todds on the two-track end of Fuller Road, and Knop on the corner of Wilson and Behling Roads.

Knop Cemetery has no fence and no gates, just stone pillars marking the entrances. One of the site's markers is a marble scroll from 1892 identifying the resting place of Henrirthe Behling. A large stone marker simply says "OTT" and a wooden sign marks the grave of William Hardt.

Walking through Todds Cemetery one has to look carefully through the flowers, bushes and brambles as many large stone markers are almost completely hidden. Three simple stones say "Mary Saunders 1879," "Sophia Saunders 1881," and "Hannah Saunders 1883."

Echo Township has two cemeteries where, until very recently, residents could obtain gravesites for free. Morehouse Cemetery has several family plots marked by cement curbs. In one, small markers face both forward and sideways. The oldest readable marker is that of J.S. & Mary A. Bartholomew, 1875. On many wooden markers, the names have long since been worn off.

Dunsmore Cemetery is off Old State Road at the Murphy Park sign. Under a bush are four stones piled together marking an unknown grave. A beautiful white marble stone is inscribed: "Our Darling; Budded on earth to bloom in heaven." "Baby" appears on the bottom. A large steeple-shaped stone is dated 1881.

South Arm Township has three cemeteries: Advance on Ridge Road, Lakeside on M-66 and Jones on the two-track Waterman Road off Bailey Road. At the Jones Cemetery, many markers appear to be cement with names written by a stick. One can just barely read the name of Seth N. Raynong, 1802 on one marker.

Lakeside Cemetery has old iron gates that stand

One would love to know the story behind this enigmatic grave marker in the St. John Nepomucene Pioneer Cemetery. *Photo by Karen Walker.*

open, overgrown with blueberry vines. One stone in the cemetery stands alone and simply says "Frankie, 1886."

Each of the cemeteries in the East Jordan area holds its own wealth of history. Some of the stones may be moss-covered and the inscriptions may be faded, but these markers still stand, proudly marking the grave of a loved one. 🦆

Law and order East Jordan style

BY TOM BREAKEY, SR.

Back in the 1930s and 40s, East Jordan was run by Chief of Police Harry Simmons and Justice of the Peace Charles J. Murphy, also known as Judge Murphy.

During their "reign," most infractions of the law were handled right here in town, swiftly and surely. Harry would find the perpetrators and arrest them, then Charlie would try them and sentence them without bothering the County Sheriff or Prosecutor.

Harry never had any formal police training but he was very proficient at his job. I'm sure most old-timers around town will be quick to agree that he was the best cop East Jordan ever had. It should also be mentioned that, in addition to his police duties which he handled alone, Harry drove the snow plow and read the water meters (he was the only one who knew where they were all located).

Gus Kitsman had built a small log cabin on the lake side of M-66 about a mile north of town when that area was nearly devoid of any buildings. Being very secluded, the cabin was a temptation to some young gaffers from town out looking for mischief. They got into the cabin and did very little damage but did help themselves to some food items which they warmed on an electric hot plate. When they left, the hot plate was left on by mistake.

The break-in was discovered and Harry was notified. He knew exactly where to look for the miscreants and promptly hauled them in for questioning. At that time, criminals were not made aware that they were entitled to have an attorney present for questioning, nor were young offenders shuttled off to Juvenile Court for coddling. So Harry proceeded to question them.

Naturally the suspects denied having been anywhere near the cabin and Harry let on that he believed their story. As the session drew to a close, however, Harry remarked, "What I don't understand is, why did you leave the hot plate turned on?" One of the kids quickly replied, "Oh, we just forgot to turn it off."

With that, it was time for Judge Murphy to do his part and, once again, justice was served in East Jordan.

The devil's buckboard

BY VIRGINIA KAAKE-GIACOMELLI

Dr. Arthur T. Bodle of Bellaire was the first person to drive a car into East Jordan. At the time these new modes of transportation were called "Horseless Carriages."

The mill at the bridge had a bed spring factory on the site of the East Jordan Lumber Company and a warehouse at the foot of Main Street. When the men in each plant saw the strange vehicle coming across the bridge, both plants promptly shut down and the crews trailed the doctor up Main Street. All business places were deserted as their owners joined the parade.

Dr. Bodle parked the car in front of Dr. Warne's Drug Store, next to the East Jordan State Bank. Mina Hite was clerking there and was about to go home for dinner. Dr. Bodle offered her a ride home.

On Main Street lived an elderly lady by the name of Hood. Her older son, Mort, lived with her. When the car came chugging erratically down the street, Mrs. Hood caught sight of it and excitedly exclaimed, "Mort, Mort come quick! The devil's buckboard is coming down the street and Mina Hite is riding in it!"

The East Jordan Co-Operative Company

BY MARIAN SHEPARD GRUTSCH

On June 18, 1918, nearly 200 East Jordan area farmers met at the Armory to organize the East Jordan Co-Operative Association. Their objective was "to secure better results in grading, packing, advertising and marketing farm products," especially potatoes.

The farmers were finding that their most important crop was also the most difficult to market. With the Co-Op, potatoes could be pooled for sale and the proceeds pro-rated among the growers. Each Co-Op member paid a $10 start-up fee and was required to endorse a $100 note to raise capital for company operations.

Since its founding, the East Jordan Co-op has reorganized two times. In 1921 members bought capital shares for $10 a share, each holding not less than five shares.

The Co-Op built the first service station in East Jordan and handled gasoline brought by rail in 8,000 gallon tankers. As the use of trucks and automobiles grew, the Co-Op saw its gasoline sales shoot upward from 100,000 gallons in 1930 to 2.5 million in 1948. A large expansion came in 1957 with the development of blended gasoline and installation of a 100,000-gallon storage tank.

At one time the Co-op hauled petroleum products to 36 dealers in Charlevoix, Antrim, Emmet, Otsego, Kalkaska, Crawford, Cheboygan, Presque Isle and Grand Traverse Counties, as well as to a bulk plant in Boyne City.

The Co-Op continued to handle much local agricultural and dairy produce. Cream was first shipped to Cadillac and starting in 1932 was sold to the local Jordan Valley Creamery, another cooperative. In 1923 the Argo mill was purchased to handle increasing grain production. Most of an excellent potato crop in 1924 was shipped out by rail but one whole boatload went to Chicago.

Reorganized again in 1937 to conform with state and federal laws, the business became the E.J. Co-Op Company. Each member received one share of preferred stock for every share of common stock, this to be redeemed in a 15-year period.

By 1942 the Co-Op was selling Farm Bureau refrigerators, radios, vacuums and washing machines. When the EJ & Southern Railroad was disbanded in

A shipment of apples and potatoes grown by East Jordan area farmers is readied. *Photo from the Portside Art and Historical Museum collection.*

1961, it handled coal which was shipped to Ellsworth and trucked to East Jordan. In 1963 the brick warehouse was remodeled, removing the barrels of oatmeal and cornmeal and the pot bellied stove around which the men used to gather.

In 1969 the original gas station burned and in 1991 local delivery of petroleum products was discontinued but the Co-Op continues today as a modern, multipurpose service center for East Jordan area residents and farmers alike.

Family dentistry spans two generations

BY JAMES SHERMAN

Dr. Charles Henry Pray moved to East Jordan from Mancelona to open his dentist office on the upper floor of the East Jordan Lumber Company building around 1904, and passed away in 1936 after a lengthy illness. At the time of his passing his son David, was graduating from high school and went on to follow in his father's footsteps. He opened an office in 1946, in the same lumber company building, on the same floor, and had to climb the same 27 steps as his father to operate his practice.

Dr. Charles Pray, DDS, was an 1899 graduate of the State University of Iowa and established his first dental office in Chicago, Illinois. Not enjoying life in the Windy City, he was attracted to Northern Michigan from an ad placed by a Dr. Porter of Petoskey.

He worked for this doctor for a couple years before going to Mancelona to open his own practice. It was there he met and married, Eva Boulard. Neighboring East Jordan was booming and it soon became apparent the town needed a dentist so in 1904, Charles and his bride moved there and he established practice.

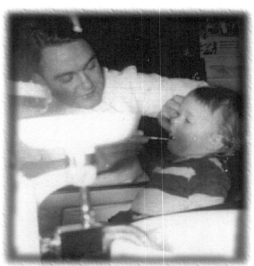

Dr. David Pray works with a young patient. *Photo courtesy of James Sherman.*

The rental cost of his first office space was $5.00 per month.

Dr. C.H. Pray became ill during February, 1933 and was sent to Mayo Brothers Clinic during a harsh winter. Dave and his brother, John, stayed home to go to school and care for their grandmother.

During this time the temperature dropped to 33 degrees below zero—giving East Jordan and the area the lowest temperature in the United States for an extended period of time.

It was so cold that water pipes and sewer mains were freezing all around town and local orchards lost many trees. Some homes from "Chemical Town" were moved across the lake to the west side during this frosty winter. The "cookie cutter" houses were built for chemical plant workers. They were moved from their location near where the vault building is now located in the East Jordan Cemetery.

Dave attended Michigan State College and, majored in chemistry before going to dental school at the University of Michigan. During his undergraduate years, he played the flute and piccolo in the Michigan State Band, which paid for his tuition of $90.00 per year. After graduating from dental school in 1942, he enlisted in the Navy Dental Corps and spent time with the 4th Marine Division in the Pacific and China.

After his war-time obligations were fulfilled, David set up practice in East Jordan in the same space as his father's office had been. In the early 1960s, he purchased a house from Clarence Healey at 306 Main Street across from the fire station and next to the GAR park. Children remember the best part of visiting Dr. Pray's office was riding the carousel horse on the front porch. The porch is remodeled and the horse gone, but pleasant memories remain.

A quiet patriot, Dave continued his work with the Navy for nearly 30 years. He retired as a commander from the Navy Reserve in 1978. Five years later he retired from private practice and turned the reins of his thriving dental business over to John Kempton.

Tragedy on Lake Charlevoix

BY GEORGE SECORD

The small motor launch Lady Margaret was no match for the 87-foot steamer Pilgrim, shown above after she was renamed Hum, when the two collided on a dark September night in 1903. *Photo from the collection of William Huckle.*

It was September 12, 1903, a day that has been labeled one of the most tragic days in East Jordan history, much the same as the Red Mill explosion. This, however, was under far different circumstances.

It began with the East Jordan baseball team in a holiday mood as they headed for a game at Harbor Springs. The day ended in death for five members of the team.

The team was owned jointly by Roy Lorraine and Harry Price. In the group, besides Harry, were Earl Bellenger, William "Kit" Carson, Frank Eckstein, Roy Gage, Lewis Hoyt, Orville Hurlburt, Seth LaValley, Joseph McCalmon, William Renard, William Shomin, Richard Steffes, Oscar Swenor, William Vought, and Fred Winters.

Harry took them to Charlevoix in his launch, the Lady Margaret, then they boarded the Pere Marquette train to Petoskey and took another boat trip across the bay to Harbor Springs. Harbor won the game 8 to 6 and our team gathered its equipment and headed for home.

Arriving in Charlevoix, Roy Gage, who was the steersman on the Great Lakes vessel Walter Crysler, decided to spend the night there. That may well have been a fatal decision. Harry said the night was very dark, with a strong wind from the southwest and a few wisps of fog. A few miles out, lights were seen, but thought to be Ironton. Roy, who was familiar with the lights along shore, would have immediately known it was a boat and steered clear.

A second fatal mistake was that, contrary to law, the Lady Margaret was running without lights and Captain Lee of the Pilgrim (later to become the Hum) never saw the launch until his vessel was virtually on top of it.

Harry was running the engine and Kit was steering. Quoting from a letter from Harry, "It is true that Kit was not familiar with marking lights. Suddenly I noticed green and red lights far apart. Grabbing a lantern and swinging it, I called to Kit to put her hard to starboard. At this instance, Captain Lee saw the lantern and signaled engineer Joseph Hyland, Jr., to stop and reverse the engines. Not more than 20 feet separated the two boats and, as the launch swung directly across the Pilgrim's bow, the latter struck almost amidships, cutting through the planking and crushing the launch like an eggshell.

"Our heavy engine carried the stern down. Fortunately, we were over a sandbar, the stern sitting on it and the buoyancy of the gas tank held the bow out of water. I, a poor swimmer, and Lew Hoyt, who couldn't swim at all, clung to the bow until picked up.

"Seth LaValley was seated in the stern. Leaping for the Pilgrim's rail, he pulled himself aboard. Earl Bellenger missed his hold and swept past but a passenger caught and pulled him aboard. Dick Steffes was thrown into the water, the big boat passing completely over him. He came up under the stern, grabbing a propeller blade, then managed to get hold of the rudder, from where he was rescued by another

passenger. Bill Shomin, an Indian, who was our catcher, was a fine swimmer. He had salvaged the grips containing the team's uniforms and swam away from the others, calling to Hyland that he could keep afloat and to take care of the others first.

"In the meantime, Hyland, realizing the Pilgrim was not seriously damaged, launched it's yawl, but someone had removed it's plug. Taking on water fast, we had to bail with hats and hands to keep afloat.

"Joe McCalmon could not swim, but Carson was a fish in the water. He was last heard admonishing everyone to keep a cool head and that he would take care of Joe. Shomin was positive Carson could not have drowned but had probably swam across the lake and would be found alive.

"The condition of the yawl made two trips necessary but Hoyt, Hurlburt, Shomin, Swenor, Vought and I were brought in safely, although engineer Hyland was so exhausted he had to be lifted aboard the steamer."

The Pilgrim cruised around for an hour before giving up the search and proceeding to Charlevoix. It returned to East Jordan at 2 a.m. with some of the survivors. Earl Bellenger was deputized to go to the Carson home and break the news to Kit's wife as gently as possible. When she came to the door, he looked at her a few seconds, then blurted, "Kit's dead!"

Sunday was a rainy day but the lifesaving crew from Charlevoix, as well as boats from East Jordan, dragged all day with zero results.

Monday morning Lew Otte, East Jordan fire chief, strung several hundred feet of rope along Main Street and attached three-pronged fish hooks suspended from heavy trolling lines to it. The rig was taken to the site, sunk with heavy weights, and drug by small open boats until all five bodies were recovered. The bodies of Carson, McCalmon, Renard and Winters were in the immediate area.

McCalmon's body was on Carson's shoulders but the heavy seas washed it back into the lake and it wasn't recovered until Tuesday afternoon. Eckstein's body had drifted nearly a mile towards Charlevoix.

Fred Winters was 30, a teacher and one of the first East Jordan high school graduates; William A. Renard was 51, a respected saloon keeper; William "Kit" Carson was known around the state as a top baseball player. He was captain of the East Jordan team which had played Harbor Springs the day of the accident and ran a bowling alley in East Jordan. Carson left a widow and three small children; Frank Eckstein, 23, was a meat cutter in Hayner's market and Joseph McCalmon, 22, was a farmer.

W.E. Malpass and the East Jordan Iron Works

BY DAVID L. KNIGHT

William Ellis Malpass was born in 1863 in the English village of Quarry, located in a section of southeast England known as the Cotswalds. His father was a shoemaker and the family operated a small farm as well.

In 1879 Malpass set out for Canada and thus joined the great wave of immigrants seeking their fortunes in the New World. After a two-month voyage across the Atlantic he landed in Quebec with the equivalent of three dollars in his pocket. Malpass continued to head west and eventually crossed the border into the U.S. at Port Huron. It was there that he met Richard Round, a foundryman, who hired him to work first in his orchard, because of young Malpass's farming skills, and later in his industrial firm, the Jackson & Round Foundry in Detroit.

As Malpass served his apprenticeship, his ties to the Round family were strengthened both through Richard Round, his mentor-employer and through Round's daughter Alice Ann, the object of young Malpass's growing affection.

Ready for another challenge, Round was drawn northward by the lumber boom. He headed for the Grand Traverse area, a focal point of lumbering activ-

William E. Malpass, right, and his brother James. *Photo from the collection of Tad Malpass.*

ity in the north, and became associated with the Traverse City Iron Works. He was followed by Malpass who found work at the Elk Rapids Iron and Chemical Co. This was in 1882 and by that time Malpass was betrothed to Alice Round. During their courtship, Malpass thought nothing of walking the 16 miles from Elk Rapids to Traverse City to visit his fiance. They were married in September of that year.

Richard Round was willing to help establish his son-in-law in a respectable business and must have had a fair degree of confidence in the 20-year old as he made Malpass a full partner in a new venture located in a fast-growing young logging town to the north named East Jordan.

The Round & Malpass Foundry was formally established by a partnership agreement signed and dated by the two principals on November 8, 1883. A copy still hangs in the lobby of the Iron Works today.

The foundry was housed in a wooden building at the foot of what is now Garfield Street. The plant's location on the South Arm waterfront provided convenient access to its primary clientele at the time, cargo vessels docked in the harbor. Also, because roads were very poor and rail service from downstate had not yet been extended to East Jordan, heavy machinery was moved by water whenever possible. Other customers for the foundry were the numerous sawmills in the Jordan Valley and local farmers who needed castings for their machinery.

As the business began to grow, the need for a machine shop became evident so William Malpass wrote to his brother James in England who was a journeyman machinist. If James would come to East Jordan, wrote William, he would build a machine shop for him. In 1886, two days after getting married, James Malpass sailed from England with his bride, Elizabeth, to join his brother's new firm.

The machine shop was added as promised. Its work at the time was primarily on log loader steam engines and saw mill parts. In the waste-not spirit of the day, power from the machine shop was sold by the Malpass brothers to an adjoining woodworking shop owned by Don Maus.

Meanwhile, Richard Round again felt the urge to move on and sold his interest in the business to the Malpass brothers in 1892.

The foundry flourished as the logging industry hit its boom years. William Malpass began to dabble in retailing with the establishment of the W.E. Malpass Hardware Store located just up the hill from the foundry. His son Charles became involved in the store and went on to operate it for many years. According to local residents who can recall the store, it carried an amazing variety of items and it was a rare occurrence when one could not find what he was looking for there.

On July 11, 1905, the obvious hazards of working with molten iron in a wooden building were borne out. The following story appeared in the July 13, 1905 Charlevoix Sentinel:

"About 7 o'clock last Wednesday, fire was discovered in the foundry of the East Jordan Iron Works and in a short time the foundry was completely ruined. They had been casting that day and the fire is supposed to have caught in some way from the cupola. The alarm was given by the steamer Hum and while the fire department responded promptly, so difficult was the laying of the hose that for the excellent work of the bucket brigade in keeping back the flames, the entire plant would have been destroyed. As it was the fire was checked in the machine shop before it had done much damage to the valuable machinery. The loss is placed at $1,000 with no insurance."

The Iron Works was immediately rebuilt with bricks made in East Jordan. For almost three decades,

William and James Malpass worked together at the Iron Works and while they may have been an effective management team, their personal relationship had a volatile side to it. "There were lots of stories about how they got along," said William "Bill" Malpass III, W.E.'s grandson who went on to become president of the company. "They got along like a couple of brothers. They argued all the time and they were pretty good at it too."

In the end, it was not only the brothers' conflicting personalities that contributed to a parting of the ways but also fundamental differences of opinion on the future of East Jordan Iron Works. Throughout his life, William E. Malpass was a visionary who, when he saw opportunity, pursued it aggressively. James was a more conservative type.

"My father wanted to progress and enlarge the foundry but Uncle Jim wished to keep it small," recalled Alice Malpass Nesman, the third youngest of William and Alice Malpass's 13 children. "We used to hear them quarreling and quarreling about Dad wanting to expand and Uncle Jim wanting to keep it small. Eventually they dissolved their partnership."

James Malpass left East Jordan Iron Works in 1917 and three years later moved to Muskegon. He continued in the iron casting industry joining the Sealed Power company in Muskegon. James and his son Ellis (who received his first name from the middle name of his uncle, William Ellis Malpass, Sr.) worked there until he retired in 1941. James died in Muskegon in 1950.

By the 1920s the East Jordan Iron Works was going through another transition, one forced by changing markets. Michigan's lumber boom was drawing to a close as the forests that once seemed endless had been all but totally harvested. As the sawmills, shingle mills, cooperages, charcoal factories and other wood product firms began to disappear, so did the lumber schooners.

For the Iron Works, the sawmills, cargo vessels and related industrial activity had been a core market. Their phase-out posed a serious challenge: either find new markets or face closure itself. Complicating the issue was the firm's location. During the logging era, East Jordan was a hub of activity but when the lumberjacks left, it's population and industrial base dwindled rapidly. Other than farmers with their equipment, there was very little demand locally for gray iron castings.

"I don't think it was any great thing for my grandfather to see the market changing," said Bill Malpass. "The fact that there were no more trees was pretty obvious." With characteristic vision, however, William Malpass saw an enormous opportunity emerging in

East Jordan Irons Works personnel pour molten iron from the cupola into a mold. *Photo from the collection of Tad Malpass.*

street castings for the Midwest's fast growing cities. Malpass was as good a salesman as he was a foundryman so he started to make regular trips to Detroit and other cities to pursue orders for EJIW-made street grates, manhole covers, fire hydrants and other castings. Many of the municipalities called upon by William Malpass are still buying EJIW castings today.

"I think he enjoyed his sales trips," said Alice Nesman. "Wherever they were having bids on something, he was there and he usually got the job. A lot of men wouldn't have the nerve to go in there and bid against many other larger firms from the city. But he was smart."

By 1928, the year that the last of East Jordan's sawmills closed, the Iron Works had made many successful inroads to the municipal casting market. Instead of boiler grates and bearing blocks for lumber mills and cargo vessels, the firm was now concentrating on the production of fire hydrants, water works valves and municipal castings for such major cities as Detroit and Chicago.

During the 1930s and 1940s, William Malpass or "Grandpa" as he became known to family and foundry employees, gradually transferred management functions at the Iron Works to three of his sons, William Henry "Will" Malpass, Richard Ward "Dick" Malpass and Theodore Edward "Ted" Malpass. A third generation of leadership, headed by Will's son, Bill

Malpass, and Ted's son, F. Bruce Malpass, emerged in the 1960s and 70s.

Half a century of foundry work took a physical toll on W.E. Malpass; he suffered two broken legs and lost an eye in the foundry. The latter incident occurred when he was pouring a mold and he had a little bit of iron left over. At the time, the foundry floor was all sand, not concrete. He poured the iron out on the floor so he could pick it up as soon as it cooled. It was near a wall in the winter time and it ran over some frozen sand, exploded and threw hot iron that burned his eye and part of his lid.

But none of his accidents ever handicapped Malpass, as far as he was concerned, or kept him away from the foundry. Even after relinquishing ownership of the Iron Works, he was at the foundry daily—to the occasional chagrin of his family.

One day in 1943, the 80-year old founder of the East Jordan Iron Works was helping tear an old wooden floor out of what was then the assembly room, preparing to put in a new concrete floor. Just as work was about to quit for the noon hour, he collapsed. A doctor was called immediately. William E. Malpass had suffered a stroke. Even this setback was not accepted passively by the indefatigable Malpass. He lost the use of one arm because of the stroke but his daughter, Alice Malpass Nesman, recalls that he continued to try to rehabilitate it by self-designed exercises, long before physical therapy was common for such conditions. Even in his partially

W.E Malpass in his later years. *Photo courtesy of the East Jordan Iron Works.*

incapacitated state, he could not stay away from the foundry. He would demand to be brought down the hill from his house at 105 E. Garfield whenever someone could be persuaded to assist him. He would sit quietly on a wooden chair in the corner, watching the operation, no doubt wishing he could be closer.

W.E. Malpass died on January 6, 1944, two days short of his 82nd birthday. An obituary in a local newspaper described him as "one of the most dominant figures in Charlevoix County."

Today, the fourth generation of the Malpass family operates what has become a leading manufacturer of utility castings for markets throughout the midwest and east. With the addition of the automated Taccone line in 1966, EJIW made a successful entry into the market for brake drums for trucks and heavy equipment. The firm has become one of Charlevoix County's largest employers, has sales offices in locations throughout the midwestern and eastern part of the country and in 1995 purchased a second foundry in Louisiana.

What is truly remarkable is that the East Jordan Iron Works has not only survived, but flourished in an industry as globally competitive as metal casting; since 1980 one of every four foundries in the U.S. has closed. But when one looks at the values, dedication and foresight that William E. Malpass instilled in the company from the outset—and which have survived fully intact among his descendants—EJIW's success is not so surprising after all.

The Belle of the Blizzard

BY MARY H. FACULAK

The Belle of the Blizzard, a creation inspired by a cold northern Michigan winter day, is one of the most delightful stories from East Jordan's past.

While the winds howled and the snow swirled around outside on a winter day in 1936, George Secord and Cyril Dolezel were inside brainstorming a solution to the frequent complaint that there was nothing to do during the cold winter weather. Thus, the idea of a Belle of the Blizzard was born.

The Belle of the Blizzard contest drew attention not only in the local Charlevoix County Herald, but was picked up by newspapers throughout the nation. Perhaps it was because of the interesting criteria for potential contestants: The girls had to be at least 16 years old and not over 21; no girl having false teeth, fallen arches, or hang nails would be considered; and contestants had to have been seen on the mill skating pond at least once during the year and be able to keep their balance with the help of no more than three people.

Eva Dennis, East Jordan's first Belle of the Blizzard in 1936, presents the key to the city to Jay Metcalf, King of Smeltium that year. To the left is East Jordan Mayor Kit Carson. *Photo from the collection of George Secord.*

Twelve contestants vied for that first title of Belle of the Blizzard. Ballot boxes were placed at the East Jordan Temple Theatre and votes were cast on the back of purchased theatre tickets.

The lucky winner would reign over the new State Street skating arena as well as represent East Jordan in area winter events.

The winner of the 1936 Belle of the Blizzard contest was Eva Dennis who received an overwhelming 110 ballots. The next two contestants garnered 63 and 34 votes respectively.

Eva received her crown and title after the East Jordan-Charlevoix basketball game. Her title read, "Miss Eva Dennis, Her Majesty, Miss Aurora Borealis, Belle of the Blizzard, Supreme Ruler of Winter Storms, Defender of the North Winds and Guardian of the Northern Lights."

The Belle of the Blizzard received a white wool snow suit and a tin crown adorned with colored cellophane jewels that had been hand-crafted by the high school shop class.

The first Belle of the Blizzard kept her title for some 55 years since for some unknown reason, the event was not held again until 1992 when the East Jordan Area Chamber of Commerce and the Sno-Blast Winter Festival organizers researched and reorganized the event and held the contest as part of the annual Sno-Blast Festival.

Seventy-two year old Eva Dennis Healy crowned her successor 55 years later as Cathleen King captured the title from a field of seven candidates. The contest is now an annual event during the Sno-Blast held during the third weekend in January in East Jordan.

While the criteria and the voting process have changed somewhat, the contest and title continue to attract the interest and respect from residents and non-residents alike each year.

Just like that cold winter day when George Secord and Cyril Dolezel dreamed up this remedy for the winter blues in 1936, the Belle of the Blizzard contest still offers the same cure during our current winter blahs and doldrums!

The resilient State Bank of East Jordan

BY HOWARD DARBEE

the years between 1926 and 1954, the State Bank of East Jordan—now FMB Northwestern Bank—went through a very interesting period of growth and development, despite facing such challenges as the end of the lumber boom, the Great Depression and the Second World War. Robert Campbell headed the bank throughout this period and when he retired in 1964, I used the occasion to compile the following summary of significant events during those tumultuous years.

Banking in East Jordan actually dates back to 1886 when George H. Martin organized a private bank in the D.C. Loveday building. In 1899 it completed its own building, where it stayed for 57 years, and in 1901 the State Bank of East Jordan was incorporated with a capitalization of $20,000.

When Mr. Campbell took the helm of the bank as cashier on June 4, 1926, the directors were George Carr, W.P. Porter, J.J. Votruba, W.E. Malpass, Fred Smith and C.H. Pray. All posting and bookkeeping was done by hand, including the posting of checking accounts. Mr. Campbell established a policy at his first director's meeting of bringing modern equipment to the bank and continued that policy throughout his career.

In 1927 a Brandt cashier was purchased and the installation of bullet proof glass was discussed. I joined the bank as a part-time helper in 1928 and after obtaining a diploma in 1930, became a full time employee. Profits were good and things went well for the bank for the next few years. It is interesting to note that the directors examined the bank twice a year in those days, a policy that continued until around 1937.

However, 1930 saw the beginning of the depression years. Profits were down, collections were hard and the bond markets dropped. The First National Bank of Boyne City closed its doors at this time. By 1931 collections were even harder and the bond market continued to drop as things steadily got worse. Minutes of directors' meetings at the time reveal a high number of charge-offs as note collections were almost impossible. The minute book also shows con-

siderable correspondence with examiners. This proved to be an extremely bad year.

In 1932 things got very much worse. There were only two people now working at the bank, Mr. Campbell and me, and wages were unbelievably low. Interest rates dropped to 3 percent. Stock assessments were considered but opposed by the directors. There were many letters from the banking department requesting that we remove certain loans and bonds from our assets and suggesting foreclosures. Replies from Mr. Campbell pleaded for leniency and more time. Deposits continued to fall, both from necessity and from people withdrawing their funds.

As the situation continued to deteriorate in 1933, we could only hope things would change—and they finally did. In August, 1933, all banks closed their doors. In looking back, I don't know how Mr. Campbell kept his mind and health during those trying years. Some of the directors who could afford it put money into the assets of the bank and we were permitted to re-open within a short time. Due to the fact that we had only two employees, it was decided to close the bank from noon to one o'clock because of the danger of hold-ups.

In 1934 interest on savings was reduced to 2 1/2 percent. When things began to look better in July, Greg Boswell joined our staff, the day after Al Capone was shot. Interest rates were reduced again to 2 percent and charge-offs continued, but business started to improve.

We started making loans again in 1935 and bought a few bonds. After everything we had been through, however, it was hard to see how Mr. Campbell had the courage and initiative to make loans and buy bonds. Business conditions continued to improve in 1936 but the banking department now urged us to remove from our assets real estate obtained by foreclosure.

Double liability for stockholders was eliminated in 1936 and for the first time in several years, recoveries exceeded charge-offs, except for bonds. My salary was raised to $100 a month.

In 1938, a small dividend was paid to stockholders,

The State Bank of East Jordan is shown at its original location at the corner of Main and Esterly Streets. *Photo from the collection of George Secord.*

the first since 1930. Also that year, the bank made application with the banking department for an Industrial Loan License. We thus became the first bank in this area to enter the field of financing cars, farm machinery and tractors. The policy of making local loans for farm machinery became one of our main sources of income.

Over the next couple years, examiners objected to our industrial loan system but Mr. Campbell, in his diplomatic but firm way, declined to change. Farm machinery continued to be good as we lined up dealerships in Charlevoix, Atwood, Ellsworth and Kalkaska.

In 1942, however, war was declared and loans virtually came to a halt. Interest rates were reduced to 1 percent. Loan activity ceased not only because of the war, but also because there was nothing to buy. The bank carried on and in 1944 opened a branch in Boyne City.

When the war ended, business activity gradually returned to normal and the bank resumed its move toward modernization. In 1947 the bank was the first in the area to purchase tellers' machines. Loan demand was very strong and when Boyne Mountain began operation in 1948, Mr. Campbell showed explicit faith in the venture.

By 1951, the bank had grown enough to warrant the purchase of property for a new building in East Jordan. Three years later, the first new bank building to be built in the city in many years was erected on Mill Street. The completion of this structure opened the bank's modern era and continues to serve the people and businesses of the East Jordan area. ↰

Note: Howard Darbee went on to become the bank's Chairman of the Board in 1967 and Greg Boswell became president. Both retired in 1975.

The Portside Art & Historical Museum

BY CYGRED RILEY

The East Jordan Portside Art & Historical Museum Society, Inc. has been registered with the State of Michigan as a non-profit organization since 1975.

The original Museum Committee was established through the East Jordan Tournament Bridge group in 1966. I served as chairman; Elaine Savory and Jane Jackson were the other members of the committee. A fund was established for the Museum and the collection began of artifacts which were stored temporarily in Huckles' store and my basement. A sum of $1,000 was earmarked for the Museum if a site could be established within three years.

We explored the possibility of restoring the Heinzelman house that had been inherited by the city but contractors said it was beyond restoration. Also, with today's regulations, a residence does not lend itself to use as a museum complex. The structure was eventually razed and the site made into the public parking lot behind Carey's market.

We then tried to acquire the East Jordan railroad depot but Howard Porter insisted that they had to keep it as an office to store their records (which are now on the second floor of the Museum). The building was sold a couple weeks later.

We investigated the Community Building which had not yet been finished at the time and which had previously housed the Post Office. We worked in conjunction with the Library Board as it needed to expand but arrangements had already been made for a youth center. By then, three years had elapsed so the Bridge group voted to spend the Museum funds on refurbishing the Children's Library.

The Portside Art Fair, shown in this sketch by Jean Harding Brown, is held each summer at Elm Pointe.

In 1972 the City of East Jordan received the gift of Elm Pointe and readily accepted the estate for public use. Harry Watson, mayor at the time, told us, "Now you can think about locating your museum."

Through the efforts of the Portside Arts organization and the Michigan Council for the Arts, we received a grant for architect-planner Victor Hogg of Williamston to do a survey of Elm Pointe and make recommendations. We were indeed fortunate to have an engineer with his reputation for historic preservation and education; Hogg had been involved in the Fort at Mackinac Island and in planning for Mackinaw City and other small towns.

In 1974 architectural plans were submitted to the City Council and heartily approved. In April, 1975 the first Elm Pointe commissioners were appointed by the Council. Later that November, council approved plans for the Museum to be located in the large building on the property known as the Lodge. Mayor at the time was Virginia Giacomelli.

The building was ideal as it needed no additional improvements to provide handicapped access. When it became known that we were ready to display artifacts and memorabilia from the area, items started pouring in. Added to the museum in 1986 was the Cyg Riley Gallery featuring contemporary works from the Portside Arts Fair Purchase Prize collection.

In 1996, the 20th anniversary year of the Museum, the challenge has become finding sufficient space for the ever-growing collection. We also hope to update our files with newer methods so we can accommodate the many varied requests we receive for information. ✒

Our remarkable Mom: Julia Gunther Rude

BY EMILY GUNTHER CLARK

Mom went to the Miles School on the corner of Miles Road and Ellsworth Road. She was one of seven children, four boys and three girls, of Gullick and Johanna Jensen.

One day, when Mom was about six years old, she got sick while walking to school with her brothers and sisters. When she got there she was so sick she could hardly stand up. The teacher sent her home about five miles in the snow. It took her hours to get home. It turned out that she had yellow jaundice.

Mom's father worked at the logging camps with his wife as a cook. Mom helped them at the logging camps when she was a teenager.

After graduating from high school, Mom went to college at Ferris Institute and then worked as a nurse at Harper Hospital in Detroit. It was there she met my father who was hospitalized with a broken leg. They married and moved to Petoskey where my father managed the A&P Store. I was born in 1923.

Before moving to East Jordan my father was a telegrapher, clerk and troubleshooter for the railroad so we moved around quite often for a few years.

The last town was Frederic where my sister Joan

Julia Gunther Rude is shown here in 1949. *Photo courtesy of Emily Clark.*

Elaine was born in 1931. The winter we lived in Frederic, Mom and I were driving to her folks' farm near Ellsworth when the car tire hit a culvert and turned over, pinning Mom in the car. We broke the windshield and I climbed through and ran down the road to a house for help. Mom had a broken neck and was in a cast from her chin to below her hips for one whole winter.

We moved to East Jordan in 1932 and bought the Painter Grocery Store on the west side at 201 Water Street, as well as the house next door. Mom worked some as a nurse for Dr. Beuker. Her life was filled with her two girls, (separated in age by eight years), six grandchildren RLDS Church and Rebecca Lodge where she went through the chairs.

Our parents divorced when I was 12 and Mom got the store. She opened the store every day at 7:00 a.m. and closed at 10:00 p.m. Her youngest sister, Josie Hall, and her two daughters helped her as clerks. She was a born businesswoman and did very well. She even helped put three girls through school, besides her own. Elaine graduated from college at Ferris Institute.

Even though we had the store, Mom continued to can and to bake bread, cakes and pies for our own use. I remember how I loved to go to the movies when I was growing up. Then as a teenager, I loved to roller skate.

When we couldn't get anyone to take us to Alba or Charlevoix or Ellsworth, Mom would close the store early and take us skating. After watching us skate until 10:00 she'd take us home and do her books for the day. She never complained.

After I married, I lived next door to Mom. One Halloween I decided to dress up in my husband's hunting clothes. I took my glasses off and pulled a nylon stocking over my head and face to go trick or treating. Mom was stationed at the side door with her bowl of candy. I went to the front door and pounded and yelled loudly, "Trick or treat." She came and put some candy in my sack.

Someone then came to the side door. When she went to answer it, I walked right into the house and sat down in a big chair in the living room. She came back and said, "Haven't you gone yet?" I said "No" in a real low voice. She asked if I needed some more candy. I said "No." She then told me I had better go (she lived alone) and she went to the phone and started dialing! I thought she was calling the police, but she was actually trying to call me.

By that time I was laughing so hard I was crying and could hardly pull the stocking off my head. I said, "It's pretty good that you don't even recognize your own daughter." We laughed together and shared hugs and kisses.

She tried to sell the store several times, but it kept coming back to her. It turned out she was in the store business for 20 years. She had an apartment built in back of the store so that when she retired she had the store front torn off and had a nice home she enjoyed for many years until her death from cancer at age 88.

My Mom was more than a mother; she was a friend, a successful business person, a community leader and, all in all, a remarkable woman. 🎗

Naming the Jordan River

BY ERNESTINE ROBERTS

As he sat, leaning against a large elm tree, sometimes in prayer, sometimes in meditation, Amos Williams fell asleep. A bearded man with an old knit cap pulled in front of his face, Amos was a preacher who traveled with his trusty horse Annabelle.

Amos had to stop due to the thick fog and dangerous terrain. As he sat he remembered the previous night and the sound of rushing water that lulled him to sleep. Amos vowed that he would find the mysterious sound of water. When he awakened the sun had burned away the dangerous fog and it was safe for him to go on.

As Amos came over the hill, there before him was the most beautiful stream he had ever seen, sparkling and splashing in the sun. Buttercups and evergreens lined either side of the stream, while fallen logs made little eddies and whirlpools with a whispering roar.

The crude map which Amos was using showed no stream, so, being a man of God, he scrawled in the name: The River Jordan.

The year was 1856 and Michigan was only 20 years old. Our country was young and in the throes of growing pains. Franklin Pierce was president and three states had seceded from the union. There was much trouble throughout the South over slavery. Here in this quiet peaceful valley, God seemed very near.

Throughout the years the river has kept the name, though the townspeople have changed it to the more casual Jordan River. It is still one of the most beautiful spots in Michigan. 🎗

Shermans: Three generations of Main Street business

BY JAMES SHERMAN

Though it has not always been a retailer of home appliances and it has not always been at its present address, the firm known today as Sherman's Appliance at 221 Main Street represents one of downtown East Jordan's longest business legacies.

The first appearance of the Sherman name on Main Street dates back 100 years to the Sherman and Son store built in 1896 at the southwest corner of Main Street, the site of the current Lumber Jack Saloon. The business was established by George Loren Sherman and his son James LeRoy Sherman, who went by the name LeRoy.

According to an old letterhead, Sherman and Son dealt in "choice groceries and meats, poultry, game, fish, fruits, provisions, tobaccos and cigars." While working in his father's business, one of LeRoy's responsibilities in the summer months was to deliver groceries to customers along the shore of the lake in his motor launch.

LeRoy went on to become very active in the East Jordan business community and was one of 102 members originating the East Jordan Board of Trade in 1907. The program of the group's first annual banquet indicates it was held at the Russell Hotel on March 5, 1908. The Board of Trade was later replaced by the East Jordan Business Men's Association.

The Sherman and Son building had groceries and

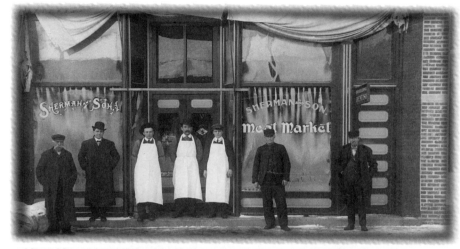

TOP: Sherman & Sons Meat Market operated from 1896 to 1911. Owner George Loren Sherman is shown here on the far left with son James LeRoy next to him. On the far right is Dr. Ramsey, a dentist whose office was on the second floor.

BOTTOM: LeRoy Sherman ran this plumbing and electrical business from 1923 to 1940. He was also one of the founding members of the East Jordan Board of Trade established in 1907. *Photos from the collection of Mr. and Mrs. James Sherman.*

meats on the main floor with the Sherman's Hall (for dances and special occasions) and a dentist office on the second floor. Sherman and Son was operated until

April, 1911 when George died. The business was purchased by Austin Bartlett and became known as Austin Bartlett's Grocery. The building was torn down in 1930 and in the 1950's Rebec's Bar—now the Lumberjack—was built on the property.

After selling the Sherman and Son store, LeRoy Sherman joined the People's State Bank which was located at the site of the present EJ Shop clothing store at 122 Main Street. He was an employee at the bank from 1912 to 1923.

LeRoy purchased the building at 221 Main St. (the current Sherman's Appliance) on May 17, 1923 from Benjamin A. Reid. He owned and operated a plumbing, heating, water works and sewers, electrical wiring and supply service in the south half of the store until 1940 and rented the north half to Blout's Variety Store. From 1940 to 1946, LeRoy Sherman provided the community with a roller skating rink.

He sold the building in 1946 to his sons George and Jim who opened a Firestone Hardware store on the site. Less than a year later George bought out his brother's interest.

George's determination to offer customers products at a good price and provide them with service when needed generated a good volume of sales. The Hotpoint Company's sales promotion program provided George and his wife Alice with opportunities to travel to many resort areas as reward for the business's high sales volume. This volume was usually accomplished by purchasing whole truck loads or boxcar loads of appliances at a time. Freight trains hauling the inventory came from Grand Rapids and would be unloaded from the tracks right behind the store.

In January, 1982 the store was sold to Jim Lercel. Retaining the century-old Sherman name, it continues to be a major appliance dealer in the East Jordan area and an anchor of the downtown retail community yet today.

The Canadian Nugget

BY JOAN SHERIDAN HOOVER

In 1948, the city of East Jordan decided to erect a memorial to the city's dead of World War II. A committee was appointed to come up with something for a memorial and was allocated $2000 to finance the project.

After some discussion and much brain racking, someone came up with the idea of hauling the "Canadian Nugget" from across Lake Charlevoix and using it for the memorial. The gigantic rock, measuring twelve feet high,

The Canadian Nugget. *Photo from the Portside Art and Historical Museum collection.*

eight feet wide, and five feet thick, was on Ellsworth Road near the city limits. According to George Secord, the rock was given its name during Prohibition.

He said going to the west side for beer was just like Detroiters going to Canada for whiskey. Hence, "Canadian" for bootlegger and "nugget" as a pun on its size.

Many people and companies tried to move "the Nugget" but to no avail. The Alpena Construction company of St. Ignace were the ones who finally moved it. Much speculation was made as to whether the bridge would hold up or not, but it did. The stone now rests in Memorial Park next to Engine #6 with a plaque on its side dedicating it to all the young men who gave their lives for our country during World War II.

Early days of law enforcement in East Jordan

BY JOE HAMMOND

In the early days, when East Jordan was known as the village of South Lake, there was no regular law enforcement other than the constable, who was either elected or appointed and had arrest powers.

In 1911 the village became a city with a charter, which provided for a Chief of Police. It appears that a man named Hank Cook was given the job because he was a large man and could handle lumberjacks and other problems that might come up on a Saturday night. During this time, much of the other police work was handled by the county sheriff.

After the passing of Hank Cook, Ole Olson was given the job for a short time and then Harry Simmons was hired. In addition to police duties, he was in charge of the streets, water and any other jobs the council came up with.

He was a staff of one so when he left town to go fishing, he would have to hire someone to fill in. In those days anyone 21 or older could be a police officer; there were no uniforms, you just showed a badge. In the summer, school teachers helped out for a small fee.

For many years, Harry had to use his own car for a police car. He earned a small fee from the State of Michigan for writing drivers licenses and also got a fee for serving civil papers from the justice of the peace, who was the local court system. There was no district court at the time.

As head of the street department, Harry would supervise sweeping of the streets with a hand broom

In the early days of East Jordan, before it became a chartered city, William Johnson, above, served as police chief, fire chief and dog warden. *Photo from the Portside Art and Historical Museum collection.*

and a barrel on wheels. He also took care of reading and repairing water meters and providing the city clerk with the billing information. Later, when the city put in a sewer plant on the west side, Dan Bennett was hired to operate the water system, giving Harry more time for police work.

As the city grew, another officer was hired to work the night shift. His name was Joe Wilkins and he was East Jordan's first uniformed police officer. Actually, he had to pay for the uniform out of his own pocket since the city council did not allocate the funds for it. Also about this time the city bought its first police car, a Chevrolet from AR Sinclair sales on the corner of Main and Mill.

I later replaced Wilkins as the night officer. Harry Simmons and Mayor Whiteford met me in my back yard one night and asked if I would take the job. I agreed to take it on a trial basis for six months. At the end of that period I told them I would stay—but only if they bought me a uniform.

I continued to work nights until Harry got sick and couldn't work any more. I was appointed chief of police and also took over the duties of the street department and other jobs that Harry still had. During this time the local police were all deputy sheriffs since the county had no full time officers other than the sheriff. Later, Philo Sumner was hired as the first full time deputy and the county bought its first car for the sheriff.

Harry W. Simmons, East Jordan police chief from 1937 to 1958, is shown in this 1951 photo with the city's first patrol car. *Photo from the collection of Jean Strehl.*

Eventually the Sheriff's Department and the city police in the county put a two-way radio system in place. Before that, however, police in East Jordan would have to watch for a red light atop City Hall which would be turned on by the hotel when there was a police call. The hotel also took fire calls and turned the siren.

In these years the closest State Police were in Gaylord and Traverse City. They came only in the case of murder or some other serious crime.

When the justice of the peace was the only local court system, one of the duties of the chief of police was to select juries for local trials. He would do this by going up and down the street, telling six people they were on the jury and had no choice but to serve.

Everything about law enforcement seemed to be a lot simpler in those days.

An East Jordan family: the Kellers, Townsends and Merediths

BY HAZEL HARTUNG COLBURN

East Jordan's heritage is marked by the stories of several families whose lives became intertwined over the years in interesting and unexpected ways. This is one of those stories.

The Keller family is traced back to Jacob Keller who was born in New York and moved with his parents to Ontario, Canada. He married Elinor Hogan, also born in New York, and the couple moved from Ontario to Romulus, Michigan. They had a son, David, who enlisted in the Union Army in 1862 at the age of 18 and was placed in Co. K, 24th Michigan, the famed Iron Brigade. They also had two other sons, Jacob Jr. and James and a daughter, Mary Ann.

After the Civil War the Kellers moved to East

Jordan and settled on Mt. Bliss Road. The house has been gone for several years but lilac bushes indicate where it once stood. Jacob donated the first piece of property for Sunset Hill Cemetery, reserving 12 plots for his family.

Before moving north to East Jordan, the Kellers' daughter met James Mattison Townsend whose family had also made its way to Michigan from Ontario. On August 28, 1862, Mary Ann Keller married James Madison Townsend in Wayne County, Michigan. They eventually followed her parents and moved to East Jordan in about 1873.

James was a carpenter by trade; his carefully kept account books are still in the possession of the family. He was very active in his trade in East Jordan and many of the houses he built are still standing. The Townsend family also helped build the Methodist Church and parsonage in 1878. James served as Village Poundmaster in 1890.

By the time James' and Mary Ann's 13th child, Nettie Ann, was born on October 10, 1883, they had lost six children, three apparently in childbirth and three from diphtheria. The Townsends later moved to a home on Mt. Bliss Road that is currently the Jerry and Linda Aydlott studio. After James Townsend died in 1898, his widow took in boarders to help make ends meet.

Nettie Townsend occupied herself by learning piano from a cousin who had taken lessons. Unfortunately the cousin died when Nettie was 13 but she had picked up enough and continued playing the piano the rest of her life. In fact, when visited by her family at Grandvue Medical Care Facility on Christmas Day, 1983, she was still able to play.

At the age of 17, Nettie was walking down the road with her boyfriend at the time, Arthur Robinson, when she spied a tall, handsome lumberjack who had recently moved to East Jordan from Benzie County. She was immediately smitten with the lumberjack, named James Edward Meredith, and the two were married on September 23, 1900. He was the son of Canadian immigrants, Cyrus Meredith and Sarah Zorena Zansbury. Nettie's mother, Mary Ann Townsend, offered the couple her home on Fifth Street in East Jordan if they would take care of her for the rest of her life. They agreed and she lived with them until her death in 1931.

In an interesting sidelight, Nettie's mother was remarried in 1915 to Aldrich Townsend, the brother of her first husband. Aldrich was a Civil War veteran who also served in the Iron Brigade and survived bullet wounds to the lung and head in the battles of Fitzhugh Crossing and North Anna.

James Meredith made a living working in sawmills and lumber camps while Nettie worked at the canning factory. East Jordan was a much different place during that era, as Nettie liked to recall. Farm animals were allowed in town and most people had outhouses; the smell could be quite overpowering on a hot day. She loved the Fourth of July and remembered walking down the maple-lined sidewalks amid the smell of fresh lemonade. Proper ladies never walked down the streets after dark because of the number of saloons and the lumberjacks out for a night on the town. Social activities included quilting bees and church functions.

Although modernization gradually crept into her life —electricity came to the Meredith home in 1917— Nettie held on to her Victorian ideals throughout her life. She called legs "limbs" and did not own a pair of slacks until she was in her 80s. She made lye soap and huge fried cakes sprinkled with sugar which she served with large cups of boiled coffee.

The Merediths had two sons, Milton and Russell. Milton was a barber in East Jordan whose first shop was in the basement of what is now the Busy Bridge shop. He played mandolin and violin, served on city council and as mayor. Russell also inherited Nettie's love of music; he played clarinet and saxophone and had his own band which performed all over the state. Several descendants of Russell and his wife Thelma still live in East Jordan. One son and both grandsons of Nettie and James Meredith were born in the house on Fifth Street in East Jordan.

After James Meredith's retirement, the couple became caretakers of the Tourist Park. Meredith Street is named for them. They continued until James' health declined. He died in 1951.

Not long after, Nettie's life took another curious turn. Arthur Robinson, Nettie's beau from her youth, had homesteaded in Red Deer, Alberta, Canada. He had married, raised a family and was widowed. He came back to Michigan and became reacquainted with Nettie. They were married at her home on Fifth Street in 1961.

However, because of problems with Social Security, Arthur was forced to go back to Canada. He wanted Nettie to go with him but she could not leave her home. She thus remained in East Jordan for the rest of her full and extraordinary life. She died on October 26, 1984 at the age of 101, having outlived both her sons, two husbands and all her brothers and sisters.

East Jordan, World War I and the American Legion

BY BILL BARNETT

In 1919, Michigan Governor Albert E. Sleeper made an appearance in East Jordan to welcome the community's war veterans home. *Photo from the collection of William Huckle.*

East Jordan's participation in World War I began with the organization of "East Jordan Military Company X." According to a newspaper account of November 29, 1913, the unit was permanently organized on Tuesday, November 25th, 1913. A bond was executed by the officers and for-warded to the State Department in Lansing. Upon receipt, arms were shipped for the entire company. The ultimate goal was to become a part of the Michigan National Guard.

Membership at the onset included Eugene Adams, Wm. Aldrich, Leon Balch, Lewis Barlow, Wm. F.

Bashaw, T. Porter Bennett (Rev.), K.O. Bisbee, Fred Bissonette, R.A. Brintnall, Fenton Bulow, Stewart Carr, A.W. Clark, Walt Cook, Junie Coon, Nelson Crandall, A.E. Cross, Jos. F. Cummins, Jack Dillon, A.W. Freiberg, Ralph Fuller, W.H. Fuller, G.E. Gainard, James Gidley, Jas. Green, Harry Gregory, Mort Handy, Carl Heinzelman, Ervin Hiatt, Clyde Hipp, Ed Kamradt, Glenn Kirby, Vivan LaCroix, Geo. M. LaValley, Harry Love, L.C. Madison, G.G. Mast, Chas. McCalmon, S.E. McGlone, Herm McMillan, Archie Menzies, J.H. Milford, Jas. Milford, Lee Murphy, M.D. Murray, Julious Nachazel, Andrew Owens, Claude Pearsall, Chas. Phillips, Hubert Pinney, Lyle Plank, Harry Potter, Harv Redson, Elmer E. Richards, Verne Richards, R.A. Risk, James Ross, Guy Sedgeman, Jas. P. Shay, Mike Shubrick, W.C. Spring, L.J. Supernaw, Len Swafford, Glenn Tomkins, Harry Valleau, F. VanSteinberg, R. VanSteinberg, Henry VanDerventer, Mose Weisman, Carl Whiteford, Dwight Wilson, Henry Winters (elected Captain), W.C. Spring, Lieut., and Walt Cook, 2nd Lieut.

Later many more would join the ranks of the officially designated "Co. I, 33d Michigan National Guard" unit: Ralph Ray Barricks, Francis "Frank" Akins, Ole Olson, Harry Beuker, Xenie Miles, Joseph Wedderburn and others.

East Jordan had the distinction of being the smallest city in the state with its own unit.

From February through April of 1916, General John "Black Jack" Pershing had been in pursuit of Pancho Villa, at this time considered a threat to peace along the Mexican-American border. His orders were to "catch or kill." A Mexican general, who was to assist in Villa's capture, instead had turned on the Americans. After refusing to take Villa when he was holed up in New Mexico, the Mexican troops actually attacked Pershing's Cavalry as it entered Mexico. Many Americans were killed and many more taken prisoner. President Wilson declared full scale war and mobilized the National Guard.

On June 23 of that year, Captain Winters, while doing some routine office duties, received a telegram from military headquarters in Lansing: "Mobilize." All National Guard units in every state were being called up for federal duty.

East Jordan's Company I was sent to Camp Grayling for training and in October they were sent to El Paso, Texas for duty with the U.S. Army and other Guard units. Though very little action was seen, East Jordan lost at least one trooper. Joe Wedderburn became ill and died there.

With the situation finally under control in April, 1917, Company I was ordered home. While en route, however, the United States entered World War I and the unit was dispatched to help guard the tunnel at Port Huron, the Detroit Water Works and Fort Wayne in Detroit.

While awaiting orders, the unit was reassigned to the U.S. Army as Headquarters Company, 125th Infantry, 32d Division. It was later to become the renowned "Red Arrow Division," the terror of the western front. In July, 1917, the reorganized unit with members now from Manistee, Charlevoix and other towns was ordered to France. As part of the American Expeditionary Force (AEF), they proved their worth over and over. Most of the men returned in July, 1919.

In 1934, they organized the "Cummins Red Arrow Group" (named for Joe Cummins who worked very hard to get them together) and held their first reunion. A gathering in 1966 still drew 13 remaining members.

This however was not East Jordan's only contribution to the military during World War I; many other men volunteered or enlisted. On July 25, 1917 a conscription (draft) call was sent out from Washington for an army of 687,000 men. In this first of possibly three calls, nearly a thousand men from Charlevoix County answered the call. Among them: Russell Barnett, Sid Sedgeman, Clinton Sedgeman, Lloyd DeShane, Albert Rebec, Louis Bathke, Merl Bingham, Chris Bulow, Roy Hammond, Harry E. Webster, Ralph Wm. Bancroft, Gaius A. Hammond, Edward Hosler, Thomas Crooks and many, many more. Some died in combat, at least one died as a result of illness from the terrible conditions at the battle front.

After the war, many of these veterans were involved in the formation of an American Legion post in East Jordan, a complete account of which can be found in "The History of Rebec-Sweet Post 227" written by Thomas St. Charles, a veteran and former Postmaster, on the 35th anniversary of the post.

The initiative began when W.C. Spring, organizer for the American Legion and former officer in Co. I, met with a group of vets in 1919 and suggested forming a post in East Jordan. The meeting went well and on December 16, 1919 a charter was authorized by the state headquarters. Officers were: A. Bruce Dickie, commander; Jos. Cummins, 1st Vice; Berl Johnson, 2nd Vice; A. F. Speltz, adjutant; Dr. H. W. Dicken, Finance Off.; Rev. A. M. Hoyt, Chaplain; Ed Kamradt, Historian.

The "Rebec-Sweet Post" was named for two comrades who paid the eternal price. The post name was

This unidentified East Jordan man posed in his U.S. Army uniform. *Photo from the Portside Art and Historical Museum collection.*

at the corner of Main and State Streets.

The event was a supper and smoke. Russell Barnett teamed up with a radio set and entertained the boys for a bit, then came an excellent oyster supper followed by coffee and cigars. The Post moved to the Town Hall in 1926 when the G.A.R. (Grand Army of the Republic Lodge) disbanded and willed all their equipment and kitchen supplies to the Post.

The next order of business was to organize an Auxiliary. In 1926, an application was made to and granted by State Headquarters, and a joint supper was held in October.

A problem came up in the spring of 1928: the building had two tenants, the Legion on the first floor and pigeons on the second. The building was condemned and new quarters had to be found. It was learned that the brick building east of the G.A.R. Park on Williams Street owned by the East Jordan Chemical Co. was for sale for $1,500.

The Post got it for $575, but a lot of fixing up was in order. Many fund raiser suppers were held including one where they served weenies and sauerkraut. It was at that dinner that something happened that the "old gang" never let Ed Kamradt forget about.

In 1934 a deal was worked out involving the theater but in 1939 it was sold back to the original owner. Later in 1939, the C.H. Whittington store building, another fix-up project, was purchased by the Post for $600. By 1944, $3,000 had been spent and East Jordan's Legionnaires were looking forward to the World War II vets heading home since they were in need of some new and younger workers.

Work on the former Whittington store was finally completed in 1947 but sorrow followed closely behind. On February 15, 1948 a fire reduced the structure to a total loss and left the Post again homeless. However, with hard work, a new Post soon rose from the ashes of the old and was completed in 1949.

The lesson that can be taken from all this: "Good soldiers never quit."

changed in the 1980s to the "Rebec-Sweet-Hosler Post 227" to honor another fallen comrade of WWI.

For its first five years the post was without a home and meetings were held at various locations. On January 19, 1925 they held their first meeting at their own quarters located above Leslie Miles' battery shop

Fire at the Red Mill, and other stories

BY VERA HIPP LALONDE STOCKER

Wreckage is shown of the Red mill, or Mill B, of the East Jordan Lumber Co. in the aftermath of the 1892 explosion and fire. *Photo from the collection of Virginia Kaake-Giacomelli.*

We lived across from the Grist Mill where the foundry now stands. The Mathers lived across the street. Mr. Mathers delivered milk and made ice cream. For 25 cents he would fill the biggest bowl you could find with ice cream.

I was five years old the second time the Red Mill burned. My mother took her hand-painted china off their rack, wrapped them in towels and gave them to my sister, Leone, who was twelve. My father Clyde came home from work a short time later and asked why Leone was running up and down the street with her arms full of china. He assured everyone if we had to leave we would, but in the meantime it was time for dinner!

During the third Red Mill fire, I was riding up Third Street with friends when we noticed an ember had fallen on Jenny and John LaLonde's barn. No one was home, so we stopped and put out the fire.

In 1929, the year after I graduated from high school, I came home from a dance in Harbor Springs with Harry Lee, the East Jordan football coach. My dad was having a poker party and they had run out of liquor. Peggy Bowman said he had snitched a bottle from fishermen he was guiding the day before and hidden it in an old stump. We all piled into the Studebaker, including me in my long black dress, and headed up the Jordan Valley. Peggy yelled "Stop!" and, like a bird-dog he headed for the stump, returning with the bottle.

As we were returning to town, the car slid off the two-log bridge and nosed into the river. Dawn was breaking as some fishermen, using logs, pried us back onto safe ground.

Harry Price: One of East Jordan's master builders

BY BARBARA ADAMS

When a town is young and starting to stretch and grow, there are always men anxious to be moving forces in its development. Harry Price, Sr. was just such a man.

Harry was born May 27, 1876, in a little log cabin located near Advance, about four and half miles from East Jordan. He was the third of Robert and Mary Esther Price's nine children. As a young man he walked a half-mile to the Two Bells School. After that building burned he attended Three Bells School located on Peninsula Road.

Though Harry never completed high school in the formal sense, he educated himself through experience and correspondence courses.

At the age of 18, Harry took a job in the lumbering business and soon went on to the building trade. His only assets at the time were a hammer and saw, some drawing paper, a strong back and boundless ambition.

Harry's first building job was as boss carpenter in the building of a house for Johnny Looze, a neighbor. He made a dollar a day. That same winter he also helped Al Brooks, a carpenter, finish an addition to his parents' house. About this time a builder named Burton E. Waterman of East Jordan asked Harry to come to work for him. He agreed and signed on with Waterman for 75 cents a day and board.

In 1897, Harry took a three-week vacation from Waterman to build an eight-room house for a neighbor, Morris Martin, near Advance. With the help of his brother Ed he completed the house in 18 days. He had contracted to build the house for $80 so after paying his brother $18 he made a profit of $62. This house is still standing.

In 1898 Harry rebuilt William Pitt Porter's house. He got this job mainly because of his ability to read blueprints. The job proved to be most helpful for the young builder as Porter was a man with a great deal of influence in East Jordan.

Harry's next job was rebuilding a house and barn for a Mr. French, a grocer who later became the president of the bank. This gave Harry another strong supporter. Later, because of these contacts, Harry was able to obtain working capital for his endeavors.

In October 1899, Harry married Grace Beers, daughter of Ammon and Jenny (Black) Beers. They had three children born in East Jordan. This marriage ended in divorce in 1919. Harry then married Pauline Thomas of Dayton, Ohio in 1931.

In 1901 he built a trestle bridge between East Jordan

One of Harry Price's early East Jordan masterpieces was the home of W.P. Porter. *Photo from the collection of George Secord.*

and the South Arm. The bridge, an 800-foot span, was supported by wooden piles and built of dismantled old steel spans he located in Charlevoix. The steel spans had to be hauled approximately 15 miles to be fit into the new structure. Waterman lent him his horses to pull the structure over the ice to its new location. The job was completed on schedule in six weeks, and turned a profit of $450 for both Harry and Waterman.

Soon after the trestle bridge job, Harry and Waterman invested their profits from the job into a successful planing mill and cabinet shop.

Another of his early important contracts was for construction of a dam and power plant on Deer Creek near East Jordan. It was the first dam Harry ever built and was the first of its type ever built of concrete in the United States.

Harry built most of the houses on both sides of the street in the 600 block of Main Street in East Jordan. At one time, immediate family and relatives occupied six of these homes. In 1904 Harry built the courthouse in Bellaire which still stands. In 1901-02 Mr. Ward needed a dock on the lake at East Jordan to enable the

Harry Price. *Photo courtesy of Barbara Adams.*

railroad to bring in lumber for transfer to barges. This was also one of Harry's projects.

Harry Price was always a man who enjoyed a challenge. For example, he built 100 frame houses in Deward in 100 days. Other projects included a brick hotel in Boyne City known as the Wolverine (now the Dilworth) and the Temple Theater on Main Street in East Jordan. The Temple opened on October 17, 1911 with the road company of Madame Sherry performing.

In 1910 Harry served on the town council in East Jordan. As a direct result of this, he paved and installed a sewer system in downtown East Jordan.

Though he eventually left East Jordan, Harry Price, Sr. continued to build and grow throughout his lifetime. He died in 1958 at the age of 82 in Dayton, Ohio, leaving behind many examples of what can be accomplished if one follows his dreams, keeps oneself physically fit, and lives each day with his eyes on the future—always building for tomorrow.

More information on the life of Harry Price, Sr. can be found in the book, "Build for Tomorrow," Copyright 1960 by Price Brothers Company, Dayton, Ohio.

Two pioneer brothers, two brave sisters

BY HELEN SPARKS

John and Charles Hott married the Garberson sisters, Arvilla and Emma respectively, in Kewanee, Indiana in the late 1800s. The two couples brought their children and cattle by train and wagon to northern Michigan and settled in the community of Afton on the East Jordan-Boyne City Road. They owned farms on Rogers, Marvin and Bergman Roads. Later there was a school, town hall and the Pearsall Store on the site. The children grew up in the East Jordan area and became homemakers, a dairyman, barber, school teacher, engineer, construction worker, telephone switchboard manager and a farmer who grew certified seed potatoes for Michigan State University.

The long lost Kingdom of Smeltium

BY VIRGINIA KAAKE-GIACOMELLI

Smelt have been a popular sport fish in Michigan since the early 1900s. But East Jordan residents gave this diminutive species special recognition when, on March 9, 1932, they organized the "National Order of Smelt."

The next year, Lewis Cornell, secretary of the East Jordan Chamber of Commerce, stated, "Can't we stage some kind of celebration during the peak of the smelt run?"

It was decided that crowning a "Smelt Queen" would be too much like other communities. Why not do something more original? The idea emerged to crown a king instead, serve a stag banquet and make it a real he-man affair.

The concept was accepted and on March 18, 1933, the first East Jordan National Smelt Jamboree was held. Al Warda, a retired vaudeville actor living near East Jordan was crowned "Albert I, King of Smeltium." The stag banquet at the Russell House had Ben East of the Grand Rapids Press for its main speaker.

East Jordan's smelt run started to become even more widely known. In 1933, B.M. Fell, a resident of Alberta, Canada, heard of the event and with his wife and daughter drove the 1,500 miles to dip smelt in the Jordan River.

Before the 1934 Jamboree, by utilizing Works Projects Administration (WPA) labor the Sportsmen's Club had built six rustic bridges, board walks along

This was an early King of Smeltium with his Queen, brandishing her royal dip net. *Photo from the collection of George Secord.*

either side of the main channel of the river and several cross walks to afford easy dipping for the thousands of people who came from downstate, out of state and the surrounding area. Many smelt dippers drove here, dipped smelt all night and then returned home the next day.

Outdoor sports writers made the event a homecoming each year. In 1938 special robes were used for the first time; previously, the Knights of Pythias had loaned theirs. The new robes were gold brocade trimmed with violet satin plastron ornamented with silver smelt and sequins. They were complemented with a Venetian red velvet cape trimmed with ermine.

The first crown had been stolen so East Jordan native Julius Nachazel of the Michigan School of Mines and Technology at Houghton had one made of pure copper with a smelt on front. The other Kings of Smeltium over its brief existence included William S. McGraw of Jackson in 1934, Jay H. Metcalf of Grand Rapids in 1935, Issac Hyams of Cincinnati in 1936, Jack Vancoevering of Detroit in 1937, George Stephensen of South Bend, Ind. in 1938, Robert Crisler of Greenville, Ohio in 1939 and Ben Wright of Alpena in 1940.

After eight years, the National Smelt Jamboree and the crowning of the King of Smeltium ran out of steam and was discontinued for lack of local cooperation. ⌣

We remember George Secord

BY GAYLE GOTTS AND JUDY MUMA

Historian, humorist, hospitable host—that was George Secord. Twinkling eyes, ready smile, quick wit—that was also George Secord. George was an unforgettable friend to many people—and he was our friend.

For decades, anyone wanting information about early days in East Jordan had only to visit George Secord, the local historian. His lively account of all aspects of the region's history was generously intertwined with amusing anecdotes. Past eras were to be relived and relished repeatedly. They were to be shared with everyone who expressed an interest in bygone days.

But George was much more than a historian and storyteller. His zest for life, both past and present, enabled him to converse about an endless variety of topics including classical music, vaudeville, politics, art, birds, stone cutting and canning peaches.

He was a self-proclaimed "railroad fiend" and discussed rail lines as though they were close friends with unique characteristics and individual personalities. The Pere Marquette was George's favorite and he boasted about it like a father bragging about his son.

Not only was George an excellent talker, he was also an active "do-er," as evidenced by the organizations in which he participated: Veterans of Foreign Wars, American Legion, Charlevoix Masonic Lodge, East Jordan Chamber of Commerce, East Jordan Portside Art and Historical Society, Crooked Tree Arts Council, Friends of Elm Pointe, Opera Guild, Michigan Oral History Association, West Michigan

George Secord as shown in a 1993 photo. *Photo courtesy of the Petoskey News Review.*

Tourist Association and Friends of Engine No. 6.

He served in the United States Army during World War II. He had an honorary degree from Western Michigan University. He owned and operated a canoe livery service in East Jordan for several years and then worked for Lear Jet until his retirement.

The Secord home, located on M-66 just north of East Jordan, was built overlooking the picturesque Monroe Creek. The home was named Sha-da-wain, Ojibwa for "trails by water." The book-filled home was a reference library for art, dance, theater, music, trains, birds and biographies. The hospitality of George and the tranquility of Sha-da-wain combined to entice many, many people to spend time in East Jordan at the Secord home.

Opera singers, professional dancers, poets, classical guitarists, fellow historians and childhood friends were overnight guests. Their lasting friendship with George was evidenced by the continual correspondence he received from each of them throughout the years.

It is fitting that a book about East Jordan should be dedicated to a gentleman whose daily life perpetuated pride in East Jordan's history. It is appropriate that East Jordan, a city filled with people of diversified interests and talents, recognizes a man who exhibited joy in expanding his knowledge on an endless variety of subjects.

It is proper that we honor the warm hospitality, the love of nature, and the gentle humor of George Secord, for it is these very same qualities that exist in East Jordan and make us proud to call it home. 🦆

Odawa of Zhingwak Ahkeh (Pine Lake Land)

BY MINUNQUA, AHNISHNAHBEH PEN NAME OF GRETA "GIGI" ANTOINE

Grandfather lowered original man from the sky world to a virtual paradise. He gave him the responsibility of naming all things that had a spark of life of the Creator within them. He also gave him the wolf to help him on his journey.

Original man, whose name was Manahbozho, and wolf became brothers. They traveled together across the earth, giving names to all of the four legged, the swimmers, the winged and the life giving plants that grew from Mother Earth.

When the journey ended Grandfather said to them, "Now you must travel on different paths. You will still be brothers, but Manahbozho must have a mate, Qua (Indian woman), to replenish the Earth."

Manahbozho and Qua learned many things from all of the beings that were named. Each one shared the knowledge that Grandfather had given them. They learned to respect all. And from the sky world, they learned the truths that they would live by.

The Odawa Muhkwa Dodem (Ottawa Bear Clan) main village was built on the shores of what is now called the South Arm of Lake Charlevoix. It was comprised of large rectangular structures topped with barrel-shaped roofs.

Constructed of wood frames covered with birch or elm bark, each building was large enough to house as many as nine families. At times the Odawa village was home to three or four hundred people. The village was also dotted with temporary conical, bark-covered tepees, which were moved as needed in the summertime to hunt, fish or gather the resources of the land along the Zeebeh (Jordan River).

The Bear Clan developed values which preserved the resources for future generations. The importance of domesticated crops, especially corn cannot be overstated. Within each village each person had an important role in procuring food and assuring the well-being of the group. Even children assumed responsibility at an early age as they imitated their parents and learned the skills necessary for survival. Young boys learned how to hunt and fish and make tools; girls learned farming and how to make clothing and other material goods.

Young Eagle was a boy, almost to manhood. He was of the Odawa Nation, Bear Clan and son of Chief Day Star. His naming ceremony was just yesterday and he was spending his first night in his own lodge. He awoke at dawn, as tired as he was when he lay down on his sleeping furs.

It had been late when he finally fell asleep. It was very strange to be alone. He had never been alone before. Oh, sometimes in the forest, when he was snaring Rabbit, he was by himself, but never in the village. He missed his father's lodge. He missed all of his brothers and sisters. He missed his father and mother and his grandfather and grandmother.

This was a very small lodge, made for him by his father and uncles. It was made of maple saplings which had been sharpened on one end and pushed into the earth to form a circle. The tops had been bent toward the center and tied with basswood fiber. Other saplings, lashed together from bottom to top, formed the skeleton of the lodge. Then, birch bark was put into place, starting at the bottom and overlapping each row until there was just a small opening at the top to form the smoke hole.

It was cozy and warm inside. Young Eagle had decorated the lodge with the gifts he had received at his naming ceremony. His shield was very colorful with the design that his father had painted on it. His deerskin shirt, breech cloth and leggings, made by his mother hung from the polished antlers that his brother had given him for just such a purpose. Beautifully seed beaded moccasins, medicine bag, knife sheath and sash adorned the lodge also.

These were his ceremonial clothes. They would be worn only on important occasions. The porcupine quilled bag for his arrows, made for him by his aunts, showed an eagle perched on the top of a tall pine tree. The bow, a gift from his uncles, stood beside it. He could now walk beside his father and his uncles as a man, instead of following behind as he did when he was a mere boy.

Medicine Bear. *Photo courtesy of Gigi Antoine.*

from the men, when they told of their time of transition from boy to man, around the sacred fire. He excitedly arose to greet the new day.

When the Tchihmo-kah-mon (long knife) came and changed this area forever, the Odawa moved on. Later some Odawa returned and purchased land back from the government. Geshiknung, great-great-great grandson of Cobmoosa's son Antione, is the hereditary, traditional chief (Ogema) of the Odawa Muhkwa Dodem. Cobmoosa died in 1865. In the powwow dances around the heartbeat-like rhythm of the sacred drum, his son crawls into the decorated skin of a bear, leading high-stepping, young Ahnishnahbeh with his solemn, ritual step.

The Odawa had no written language. They kept their history alive with storytellers telling the stories of the past. These stories would be repeated many times, word for word, so that none of the rich traditional cultural and spiritual values would be lost. They are still being told today.

The Ahnishnahbeh (Native American) is still here in this place we call Zhingwak Akeh. We love this land just like you

As Young Eagle slipped an arm from the warmth of the furs to put some kindling on the fire, he thought of the lessons that he would learn today. Today was his time in the forest alone. He would use all that he had learned of East Jordan love it, and we are happy to share a small portion of our history.   🦆

Stories in this account are taken with permission from the manuscript Medicine Bear by Minunqua (Blueberry Woman).

Snowmobiling in East Jordan

BY TOM GALMORE

Snowmobiling started in one form or another in the early 1900s. The first production model was a kit built for a Model T Ford in 1913. Some of these were used in the East Jordan area, most notably by some of the mail carriers.

The kit consisted of a pair of wheels mounted to the rear of the car, two endless tracks, a pair of skis and a step with the word "snowmobile" on it. There is a ski and a step from one of those kits at the East Jordan Snowmobile Club located on Mt. Bliss Road south of Rogers Road. The step is cemented into the fireplace to hold the stove poker.

A.D. Graham has one of the original snowmobile kits for his Model T and has displayed it in parades.

Shown on this early snowmobile are Carl Petrie at the wheel and Joyce (Petrie) McDowell outside. *Photo from the collection of Wilma Zoulek.*

The first snowmobile dealer in East Jordan was the E.J. Auto Parts. They sold a machine called a Trail Maker, starting in the winter of 1962-63. A Mr. Scott in Ironton sold Polaris snowmobiles at about the same time. Julius O'Brien, a DNR officer, was the first person in town to own one of these models, an eight-horsepower Polaris Voyager.

In the 1960s and 70s there were over 100 different brands of snowmobiles manufactured but by the mid-1980s only four were left: Arctic Cat, Polaris, Ski Doo and Yamaha.

Snowmobiling became a major family sport in the 1960s. The East Jordan Snowmobile Club started to get organized in 1966-67. In 1968 the group purchased 30 acres of land from Bill and Muriel Zoulek for a clubhouse. On Labor Day of that year club members started construction.

The club's first money-making project was a grass drag race in Tom and Mary Lou Breakey's field at the west end of Cooperage Street. The race was held on July 4, 1967; it attracted plenty of racers and a large crowd. The club also sponsored a race on the lake at the Tourist Park that year and Dort Gibbard also pro-moted a race at the old fair grounds where there was an oval.

Cross country and powder puff racing events were included at the fair grounds and a number of women participated. In the winter of 1967-68 the club sponsored a race at the corner of M-66 and Nelson Road. It was moved there at the last minute because there was too much slush on the lake to race. A food concession was set up in Basil Crawford's garage as a fund raiser. The club has continued to sponsor races, most of which have been held at the clubhouse.

For several years the East Jordan Snowmobile Club grounds were home to the Michigan Snowmobile Association. The offices were housed in a Boyne Falls Log Home A-frame built at the front of the property. After a few years the MSA became primarily involved in racing and the name was changed to the Michigan International Racing Association. The group eventually relocated its headquarters downstate and the A-frame was sold.

The East Jordan Snowmobile Club continues to be active. Their clubhouse is used for a variety of organization and community activities. 🐦

The Peninsula Grange

BY MARIAN SHEPARD GRUTSCH

In the 1840s farmers realized that although they comprised 90 percent of the population, they were not being represented by politicians because they were not organized. After the Civil War they joined together in a statement of rural independence. Through the Grange, farmers pushed for equality with city business, for rural mail delivery, rural electrification and other common causes. Today the Grange is still a catalyst for positive change in the community and a stable, family orientation.

In August, 1895 the Peninsula Grange in the community known as DeWhite received its charter as the 706th in Michigan. Land was leased for 99 years for $1.00 from Bert and Robert Price, lumber was donated by Samuel Parsons and George Chaddock, and the hall was built on Looze Road in 1896 through the efforts of an enthusiastic membership after the harvest.

Dances, card parties, educational programs, concerts, community meetings, pot lucks and fund raisers have all been held over the years. The hall has also seen many family reunions, weddings and Christmas parties. During the Depression, Grange members made sure needy neighbors had firewood. Oyster suppers were held in the 40's to benefit polio victims.

Of the 15 granges once active in Northern Michigan, only the Barnard Grange and the Peninsula Grange remain. In 1995, at the 100th anniversary of the Peninsula Grange, there were six Gold Sheaf members with over 50 years of Grange service, they are members of the Grutsch, Luebke, Leu and Murphy families. 🐦

The East Jordan Chemical Plant and Blast Furnace

BY NORM BARTLETT

Shown here from its wood yard, the East Jordan Chemical Plant and Iron Furnace dominated the city's waterfront at its height. *Photo from the Portside Art and Historical Museum collection.*

Plans for the East Jordan Chemical Plant emerged in 1907. Capital for the venture included financing from sources in both East Jordan and Boyne City. As construction got underway at a site on Lake Charlevoix, bricks and

steel were brought in to build the blast furnace and hot-air heating stacks.

The plant opened in 1909 with a six-story distillery, warehouses, eight retort ovens to char hardwood, and three rail locomotives. According to the International

Encyclopedia of 1913, the East Jordan Chemical Plant and Iron Furnace was not only the most modern and up-to-date plant of its kind in the world, but the largest!

Local hardwood tree tops and scrub sizes were used to make charcoal. Wood shipped in by rail was cut to four-foot lengths, then split to 6 to 8-inch widths. John Lucey's gang of 12 strong men managed the wood, stacking it atop raised-earth windrows. A narrow-gauge donkey train moved through the 2,000-cord yard with wire side buggies as the men rotated the green wood for a year of drying.

Retort ovens used to make the dry wood into charcoal had to be nearly airtight. Volatile vapors were captured during this process and converted in the distillery to wood alcohol and a brown granular acetate of lime which required raking and turning. This was a hot, eye-irritating and suffocating operation.

The capability to produce these by-products allowed the EJ Chemical Plant's blast furnace to continue operating even after four other area furnaces in Ironton, Boyne City, Mancelona and Elk Rapids had to close when wood for charcoal became scarce. It took about six cords of wood a day to raise the blast furnace to the 2,800 degrees necessary to melt iron ore. Two and a half four-foot by four-foot by eight-foot cords melted one ton of iron. At the Chemical Plant, each cord also produced two and a half gallons of wood alcohol and 125 pounds of acetate.

Ore was shipped in by boat from Escanaba at one dollar a ton. Shipping ore by rail would have cost four dollars a ton. The ore was only 30 percent iron so the remaining sand and waste had to be dumped in low land around the lake, causing the water to smell of chemicals. City roads were built with the cinders which made for rough riding from the frost-heave of winter and sooty dust in summer.

Unlike the East Jordan Iron Works cupola, the Chemical Plant's blast furnace was capped and the heat and smoke diverted to an outside chimney. A big steam engine forced charcoal-heated air in from two brick stoves to separate the ore. There were two casting pours of iron a day, one at 3 a.m. and the other at 3 p.m., each of approximately 20 tons.

Two ships, Venezuela and Griffon, carried ore in and cast iron ingots out. The largest shipment to move through the channel at Charlevoix was 3,200 tons.

Much of the labor for the plant came from Tennessee and Kentucky. At its peak the plant employed 400 men at 17 cents an hour, or about $55 a month. They worked a 12-hour day, 84 hours in a seven-day week. Car loading and wood cutting was done on a piece work basis. A split cord brought ninety cents. A ton of iron ingots loaded onto gondola rail cars paid nine cents, which amounted to about one cent per four, 75-pound cast pigs carried up a plank and dumped!

People did not complain then because they knew of little but survival. Some men lived in shacks along the tracks and some walked into work from up to three miles out of town. The bosses lived in houses on the hill overlooking the plant.

Two schoolmates of mine worked at the Chemical Plant, Chester Amburgy and Allen Green. Allen was killed in 1925 when he was run over by an ore buggy.

The plant workers used humor on the job to survive. Men who formed sand molds were called "sand hogs." John Lucey's men were the "cotton-tail gang" because of the rabbits in their yard. A center channel for molten iron flowing from the tapped porthole of the furnace into the casting room was called the "old sow."

The molten iron was diverted by a man with a wide spade as it flowed into the sand molds to form the ingots, called pig iron. Sparks would fly everywhere as one side of the casting room was poured. The other side would be poured from the next batch. The place where the pigs were piled was called the "pig yard."

The plant's busy years made millionaires of its owners. But things changed in the 1920s when coke became more efficient for firing blast furnaces and big lakers began shipping ore from the huge Mesabi Range of northern Minnesota directly to Detroit. There were other setbacks as well; strikes crippled production in 1925 and the ovens were destroyed twice by fire. The plant finally closed in 1927.

When the plant closed, bricks and other materials were sold for next to nothing as salvage since times were hard. The footings of the Chemical Plant can still be located on Lake Charlevoix below the cemetery. Part of the site was used in the 1950s as a marina, fenced with the cat-walk used when the cables were spun for the Mackinaw Bridge.

East Jordan has seen many successful industries over its history, but few had as a strong an impact on the community during its peak years as the Chemical Plant.

My life in nursing

BY WILMA SCHROEDER ZOULEK

It was my Grandfather Shroeder's nurse who impressed me so much with her knowledge of how to care for him that I decided, at the age of seven, to be a nurse when I grew up.

Before entering nurse's training I was a teacher's aid for Miss Clark who had 60 pupils in her sixth grade. In January, 1930 I began a three-year nurse's training course at Henry Ford Hospital in Detroit. Shortly after I began, I received a package containing 60 letters from Miss Clark's sixth grade pupils.

They were all graded from "A" to "fair". I was delighted and would have loved to give each pupil an "A" for their effort.

During my three years training I had many new experiences. In one, I delivered a baby girl to a Mrs. Smith before the doctor got to the delivery room. All went well. Imagine my surprise when the parents named the baby Wilma Clara after me and Clara (Mrs. Henry) Ford. Wilma Clara Smith would be 63 years old now. I wish I had kept in touch with this family.

I graduated from nurses training in 1933. Henry and Clara Ford attended our graduation. Henry Ford presented each of us with our Henry Ford Hospital Nursing School Diploma. Clara Ford gave us our Henry Ford Hospital Nurse's Pin. In May, 1933 I passed the State Board Examination and became a registered nurse. I continued to work as a registered nurse at the Henry Ford Hospital.

I married Fred Zoulek in 1935 and the next year Fred and I moved to the 80-acre farm where I still live. It is located on Schroeder Road five miles south of East Jordan.

When needed as a nurse, I went to neighbors' homes as well as other area homes to care for the sick. Many babies were born at home then. I remember the following women for whom I was present at the births

This portrait of Wilma Schroeder Zoulek in her nurse's uniform was taken in May, 1933 following her graduation from Henry Ford Hospital in Detroit, where she received her diploma from Henry Ford himself. *Photo from the collection of Wilma Zoulek.*

of their babies in their homes: Frances Hayward, Belle Sweet, Eva Hartung, Zella Lewis, D. Gibbard, Alta Hayward and Dorothy Schmitt.

On one day in January, a pregnant woman about to

deliver set out for home from the doctor's office, accompanied by the doctor and her husband. The last part of the way to the home, however, was full of snow. The woman's husband had made a snowmobile with ski-like runners on the front and a track on the back; it had only one seat. This was occupied by the husband, patient and doctor so when they stopped to pick me up, I had to sit on the doctor's lap. The doctor, with his Irish humor, remarked, "Well, there is a first time for everything. It's the first time I had my arm around my patient and my nurse on my knee at same time."

When we got to the couple's home, the husband held an oil lamp so the doctor could see to deliver a baby girl around 9 p.m. I gave the anaesthetic. I stayed at this home all night and slept with my patient; holding the baby cuddled up to me for warmth because she cried from cold when left in her crib. After all, she had just arrived from a much warmer climate!

Another patient I nursed in his home was William Malpass, founder of the East Jordan Iron Works. He was a nice old gentleman and liked to reminisce about his boyhood in England. One day he smiled

and said to me, "I married around."

"Oh?...," I replied.

"Yes, my wife's maiden name was Round," he said.

Other patients were Agnes and Carrie Porter. Agnes worked in a store, Carrie was a retired school teacher. Their brother William was a retired lumberman and lived in a large house which today is used as an adult foster care home.

I worked 15 years at Charlevoix Hospital and spent ten years as a Public Health nurse in Antrim County. It's population then was 10,000 and of these, 3,000 were school children. Of the eight schools in the county—Ellsworth, Ellsworth Christian, Central Lake, Mancelona, Alba, Alden, Bellaire and Elk Rapids—I visited each once a week. Anyone who wished to see me during a school visit left a note for me in the school's office.

I get pleasure now when men and women come up to me end say, "Hello, Mrs. Zoulek. You used to come to my school and sometimes my home."

I reply, "Please tell me who you are because you have grown up, while I have grown only gray hair and wrinkles."

Lessons learned, and some not

BY TOM BREAKEY, SR.

Andy Aikens was one of the many colorful characters of East Jordan's past. Andy, it seems, spent most of his time in the local taverns. He was usually in the company of two buddies from across the lake named Frank Lamieux and George Bear.

Every month on Social Security check day, Frank and George would come across the bridge to the Post Office, pick up their checks and proceed to the local watering holes. One time, while wobbling his way home across the bridge, Frank wandered out on a dock and fell in the lake. He was found the next morning right where he fell in.

It was quite a loss to George and Andy, but not enough to interfere with their routine. One month to the day after Frank drowned, George fell off the bridge on his way home and went to join Frank in that Big Saloon in the Sky.

Andy happened by shortly after George was hauled out of the lake. Police Chief Harry Simmons, hoping to make an impression on Andy, said "See what happens when you get too much beer?"

Andy sized up the situation and said, shaking his head, "Uh, uh. Not too much beer. Too much water."

The lasting legacy of D.C. Loveday & Son

BY PEGGY LOVEDAY MCKENZIE MIDENER

If you look at old turn-of-the-century pictures of Main Street in East Jordan you will see a very bustling town: heavy foot and horse traffic, buildings from corner to corner for three blocks, no empty store fronts, no "for sale" signs. It was a heady time for enterprising people interested in starting up businesses and creating a town able to keep pace with the times.

My great grandfather, Douglas Charles Loveday, arrived in East Jordan in 1883 with his wife and three children. There had been six children but three died at an early age. The Lovedays wanted to settle down in an area that offered all the attributes one looked for in maintaining good health and prosperity: invigorating fresh air, sparkling clean waters, great natural beauty and opportunities to contribute to a growing new community.

Douglas C. was born in England in 1840 and came to America with his parents, brothers, and sisters when he was ten years old. They resided in the Chicago area where he absorbed and enjoyed the best of both English and American cultures. It was this part of his background that helps one understand his desire to smooth some of the rough edges of a vigorous and sometimes rowdy northern Michigan town.

Within 20 years of his arrival in East Jordan D.C. Loveday established a successful hardware business, built the Loveday Opera House, erected the first brick residences in the town (including his own), organized and built the first power and light company, served

TOP: Douglas C. Loveday.

BOTTOM: W. Asa Loveday. *Photos from the Portside Art and Historical Museum collection.*

two terms on the village council, was first to build a brick building on Main Street, put in a steam heating plant and was first to build cement sidewalks. In addition, he secured the Chicago boat service and was agent of the boat company, even docking the boats.

In December, 1903, he moved from his downtown apartment over the hardware store into the spacious, English-style brick home he built on the Nichols Street hill, between Main and Second streets. But it was a sad move because his dear wife of 40 years, Caroline Weller, died in April of the same year and was never able to share the home they planned together for so long.

Their eldest daughter, Maude, had died nine years before so that left Louisa, the youngest, to share the big home with her father. D.C.'s son, W. Asa Loveday, had been married in 1892 to Mayme Boosinger, sister of one of East Jordan's leading merchants, and had a family and home of his own.

In 1884, D.C. Loveday was appointed executor of his late father's estate which entailed frequent trips to Chicago and four trips to England before his father's affairs were settled. He turned over his business responsibilities to my grandfather, W. Asa, who, in his early 20s began his own career of juggling the maintenance of a successful hardware business and tending the Opera House bookings and daily management. He later added a real estate agency to his tasks and also found time to be president of the

Work on the Tourist Park, obtained by the city largely through the efforts of Asa Loveday, is shown here in 1927. *Photo from the Portside Art and Historical Museum collection.*

East Jordan Village Council from 1897 to 1899. The Board of Trade, forerunner of the Chamber of Commerce, was organized in August, 1903 and he became its first president.

He devoted great time and effort promoting East Jordan and the surrounding area and wrote a wonderful advertising piece extolling the unexcelled conditions for successful farming or anything else to which an industrious person might put his hand on. Copies of this brochure can be seen today at the East Jordan historical museum.

Because of his efforts, the site of our present Tourist Park was made available through negotiation with the Ward estates of the Deward lumbering empire. This resulted in my grandfather's purchase of the lakefront properties, securing of the rail road rights, and clearing of the title so the city could buy the whole area for $500.

It was a hard sell. The city fathers delayed action on the proposal and the original plan for developing one mile of lakefront land as a tourist and resort area ended when investors in the plan wearied of the inaction and went elsewhere.

A year of patient correspondence with all parties involved finally resulted in the Tourist Park property being owned and maintained by the city. This finally took place in 1925, much to the relief of my grandfather, who wanted so badly to make East Jordan an attraction that would eventually encourage people to buy and settle in the area.

A series of tragic occurrences followed, brought on by bad luck as much as anything, and slowly the Lovedays' prosperous endeavors in East Jordan—and their many influences on the town—began to erode. In 1907 a season of unusually heavy rains caused a break in the dam at Deer Creek which had provided additional power to the electric plant in town built by D. C. and W. Asa Loveday in 1892. They sold the plant in 1910. In April, 1910 the Opera House was destroyed by fire. Finally, the Great Depression of 1929 wiped out most of the family's remaining assets.

My grandfather worked hard the rest of his life trying to sell property in a scarce market and promoting the potentials of East Jordan. He died in 1946. He would have died all over again if he could have seen what lakefront property is selling for now!

The house on Nichols Street still belongs to the family and is lovingly cared for and shared by descendants, now in the sixth generation. Loveday is a name we are proud to remind people of. It once made a big difference in East Jordan.

My friend George

BY JOAN SHERIDAN HOOVER

When I first met George Secord in 1975 he had recently retired and I was a senior in high school. The "ladies at the library" referred me to him because he was considered the authority on local history and I was writing a term paper for English and Government on the history of East Jordan. George and I became fast friends and, over the ensuing 20 years until his death, we shared many experiences that still give me a "warm fuzzy" feeling.

In writing my term paper, he helped me with resources ranging from old books to the gift and loan of photos from his archives. I read his mother's "Looking Backward" columns that were carefully preserved, each pasted to the page of turn-of-the-century books. One was an agricultural statistics book, if I remember correctly.

George was never satisfied with his knowledge, so as I worked on my history, he worked on filling gaps in his "data base." I remember poring over old maps, new maps and books to help him locate old cemeteries. Once we identified them on paper, we would hop into his station wagon and find them. These old plots were often

George Secord is shown here in a mid-1980s photo, had an insatiable appetite for local history. *Photo courtesy of Lynn Carson.*

overgrown and hidden, but always exciting—at least from our perspective.

On these cemetery expeditions we also were gathering stones for the front of his home, Sha-da-wain. I remember calling him on the phone and saying, "George, I found a great rock pile," and we'd be off on another adventure. Watching him build the wall (which he learned how to do from watching his contractor build his stone fireplace), was a joy. He'd evaluate each stone for size and shape and then wet it down to make sure it was pretty enough. He did a good job.

When I joined the Navy, George was a faithful correspondent. When I came home on leave, he would bring out the Earl Grey and Grandma Edward's cookies (recipe at the end of this story), wind up the Victrola and tell me about his Navy adventures—from the perspective of an Army private. During his wartime duty George spent a lot of time being transported on ships; he talked about going through the Panama Canal and crossing the Equator.

In spite of nearly 50 years difference in our ages, it was never a chore to visit George. My mother called him my "old boyfriend" he called me "Joanie-Girl." Our last big expedition was in the late 1980s, when we went exploring to find Deward. Anyone who knew George knows how important Deward was to him. He was born there and loved to tell the story of a town that sprouted up on the Ausable for just 12 years to harvest the cork pine and other lumber in the area.

Visiting this scenic spot on the river was made real through George's vast photo collection of Deward. With the help of the photos and George's memories we were able to find the location of the mill and the general store. It was here that Grandma Edwards dispensed her white cookies to lumberjacks, visiting salesmen and lumber buyers, and children alike.

All that remains of Deward, which was located east of Mancelona, are a few bricks and piles of concrete to indicate that this peaceful spot was once a thriving lumber town.

I didn't see George as much in his later years, but my memory of him is still strong. I like to remember autumn days on the back porch, sitting on a lounge chair sipping tea and hearing George tell the stories behind his interior decorations: an Indian club, the old Victrola, ancient skis and snowshoes, and the seemingly never-ending supply of pictures and memories. George was a special friend.

One of George Secord's passions was the railroad. Shown in this photo is John, Howard and Donald Porter with the old No. 6 steam locomotive of the East Jordan & Southern Railroad which they presented to the city in memory of their father, W.P. Porter, founder of the railroad. The engine still resides on the the East Jordan waterfront today. *Photo from the collection of Jody Clark.*

Grandma Edwards' White Cookies

2 cups Sugar	*1 tsp. Soda*
1 cup Shortening	*2 tsps. Cream of Tarter*
3 Eggs	*1 tsp. Salt*
1/2 cup Sweet Milk	*1/2 tsps Mace*
4 cups Flour	

After taking from oven, sprinkle sugar (from a salt shaker) lightly over the cookies

(as typed by George Secord)

Additional comments for the modern baker: Cream sugar and shortening together, add eggs and milk (I use whatever milk is on hand). Mix dry ingredients separately, then add slowly to wet ones. Roll into balls about the diameter of a quarter and place fairly far apart on an ungreased baking sheet. Bake for 8 to 10 minutes in a 400 degree oven. Don't expect them to stick around long, because they are really good!

The family of George Kitson

BY JANICE M. PREVOST VIEAU

George Kitson was born November 23, 1820 in Knapton, near Leeds, England, the son of William and Joanna Jackson Kitson. George, along with his three brothers, Jonathon, William, and John, traveled to Canada in 1854 and settled in Kent County, Ontario.

An interesting thing about this family is that two brothers married two sisters. William Kitson married Annie Sissons and George Kitson married Mary Ann Sissons. Both marriages took place in Kent County, Ontario, in 1855.

It wasn't long before distance would separate these two families. Thomas and Ellen McKay Sissons, the parents of Mary Ann and Annie, would move to Portage La Prairie, Manitoba. I believe that the Sissons were some of the earliest settlers in that area. William and Annie Kitson followed them and settled there also.

George and Mary Ann Kitson stayed in Kent County, Ontario, where George worked in a lumber mill as well as keeping an active farm with sheep, horses and bee hives. George and Mary Ann had ten children, five were born in Ontario. They were Thomas William, John Alexander, Lorenzo Dow, Jonathon, and Georgia Ellen.

Between 1865 and 1869, the Kitson family moved to East Jordan. Some cousins and other family members remained in Western Michigan also.

Some wonder if George and Mary Ann were on their way to Manitoba and the wheel fell off the wagon so they just stayed in Michigan. I believe that it was the lumbering era that led them to and kept them in Michigan. George and his sons were experienced sawyers and had worked in sawmills before. On July 29, 1869 Mary Ann gave birth to Daniel Samuel. Kate Elizabeth, Samuel Howard, Anna Willena, and Arthur Harold were also born in East Jordan.

Some of the older children would leave East Jordan and venture out to Western Canada and to Riding Mountain, Manitoba. But George and Mary Ann stayed on. They probably visited Canada, as relatives there remembered George as a "dapper man in a Prince Albert coat and a Bowler hat."

The Kitsons lived in and possibly built the now-abandoned house that sits on Metz Road today, not far from the corner of Ranney Road. The County of Charlevoix Plat book from 1901 shows that George owned 80 acres in South Arm Township adjoining that of George Ruggles and H. A. Blanchurd.

They were a busy family with all the comings and goings of their family members. They were also a caring family who took in homeless children from time to time. Odessa Hadley was one of those children. Her daughter remembers how one day Odessa and Grandma Kitson, as Mary Ann became known, were out traveling in the buggy when a new horseless carriage came along. The startled horse bolted and tipped the buggy. When the driver realized that Grandma Kitson had broken her collarbone, he said he knew a lady who would help her until she could manage by herself. Odessa remembered seeing a lady coming across the field with her children. That lady was Ida Cleland, a widow, and the children were Marjorie, Viola and Harold. Ida would later marry Dan Kitson and live in that same house.

On June 27, 1901 George Kitson died at the age of 82 of heart failure. He was buried in the Hipp Cemetery by undertaker H. Whittington. George's grave is now in the Lakeside Cemetery and is easily visible from the road. It is believed that all his children came to East Jordan for the funeral, some having to travel great distances.

Kate Elizabeth Kitson, the oldest East Jordan born child, kept house in Charlevoix for some time before traveling to Portage La Prairie, Manitoba for a year or so. She married John Lewis Kribbs, a river boat gambler-type. Her brothers quickly had the marriage annulled and nothing was ever heard of this Mr. Kribbs again.

Kate returned to East Jordan and lived at home with her mother and brother Dan and his family. She married Dennis E. Allyn, a day laborer, and had five children.

Samuel Howard and Arthur Harold Kitson both moved to Manitoba when they were of age. It is believed that they would have a better chance of having their own farms there. Georgia Ellen Kitson married Duane Cyril Tyler, son of John and Hannah Dir Tyler, in East Jordan in 1888. Tyler came from the Kalamazoo area to work in the mills. Within a year or so, they also left for Manitoba.

Anna Kitson, the youngest daughter, married a man named Crothers and lived in Detroit. Nothing more is known of Anna except that her eldest son's name was Ervin, and her son Howard had a position on the School Board of Detroit.

As the years passed, Grandma Kitson slowly went blind. Dan and Ida Kitson always took care of her. In her later years, she still knitted and loved to have her grandchildren read to her. In 1914, Dan Kitson started the process of moving his family and his mother to Manitoba. Several articles in the East Jordan Herald tell of the many receptions at the Grange for the Kitsons before they left.

Miss Marjorie Cleland and Mr. Orvis spent Sunday evenings at the home of Mr. Secord. Most likely playing piano duets. George Secord told me of the many duets his mother had with the Cleland children.

In March of 1914, a large auction was held at the farm of Daniel Kitson. In April of that same year, Dan left with a carload of household goods. His children Velma, Glen and Woulena, his wife Ida, her children, Marjorie, Viola and Harold Cleland and his mother Mary Ann Kitson would follow him the next week to Riding Mountain, Manitoba.

Daniel took all the flooring needed for a brand new house with him and, as rumor had it, the new home was the envy of Canadian homeowners in the area. He would write letters from time to time to his old friends in East Jordan, but would never return.

Grandma Kitson was my great-grandmother. My father was Kate Kitson Allyn's first child, Edgar. Even though the family of George and Mary Ann Kitson have been gone from the area for over eighty years, East Jordan was their home and they were very happy there.

Many of my family have visited East Jordan and walked around the old farm and grounds. Today it stands deserted and empty. We've been told that no one has lived there since the early 1940's. There are no windows, and nothing left of the Kitson's inside or out. Brush and trees have overgrown the land. The old barn lies in a collapsed pile of ruins. What once was a well worn path from the road to the house is today barely walkable; the weeds are waist high and there are terrible ruts.

But long ago, one could see wagons and buggies coming up the drive, and an active household with many children running and playing in the front yard of the sparkling white house. Behind were men, busy in the fields. Uncle Dan would be getting honey from his many hives, Great Grandma Mary Ann would be hanging clothes with grandchildren playing at her feet. In the big tree out front would be Edgar and his brothers looking far to the banks of the Pine River that flows into Lake Charlevoix. Such was life in the early 1900s at the farm of George Kitson.

John Seiler's "Big Jug Farm"

BY JODY MALPASS CLARK

People by the hundreds used to stop at John Seiler's farm on the edge of East Jordan to ask about the two huge jugs standing in the front yard. And John, recalls his son Parker, would have a story ready for them.

"Dad would tell everyone he brought the big jugs home to the States when he left India, where he was born the son of Presbyterian missionaries," said Parker. "He would say that he found them while on a marvelous trip through far Arabia which ended in East Jordan, Michigan. Of course, he would add that the jugs were the ones in which Ali Baba's 40 Thieves hid!"

Ironically, children do now hide in the one surviving jug Parker Seiler has in his own front yard.

John and Cora Seiler, above, enjoyed telling marvelous stories about the huge jugs that sat at the entrance to their property for many years. *Photo courtesy of Parker Seiler.*

After spinning his yarn for inquiring visitors, John Seiler would eventually give in and tell the real story of the jugs. The fact is, it is almost as interesting as the made-up one. The jugs were made by the General Ceramic Co. of New York City in December, 1920. Each stood about five feet high, weighed 544 pounds and could hold 264 gallons. They were purchased by the East Jordan Chemical Plant for $140 apiece to store acid, but the plant never did use them.

John Seiler purchased three of the jugs in 1930 for a total of $15 and placed two of them on the highway in front of his property which became known as the "Big Jug Farm." In 1936 one of the jugs was sent to the University of Michigan in Ann Arbor which had a furious rivalry with the University of Minnesota over the "Little Brown Jug" trophy. For a number of years the U of M used Seiler's giant jug as part of its halftime show during the Michigan/Minnesota game.

The history of another of the jugs was not as pleasant. After standing on the highway for over 50 years, a drunk driver smashed it to smithereens. Fortunately, the driver was not hurt but the insurance company gave Seiler $1,000 instead of attempting to replace the original. Not bad on a $5 investment!

Early days of fishing guides on the Jordan River

BY THORA KOTOWICH

The Jordan River is considered one of the highest quality streams in Michigan's Lower Peninsula. With its dense wilderness, majestic scenery and rapidly flowing water it became the ultimate for trout fishing and canoeing.

Some early fishing guides were Austin and Orin Bartlett and Bob Proctor. Sixteen-foot flat-bottomed johnboats were used with heavy drag chains. They were propelled by the guide from the back of the boat using a pike pole. Few people could push and control the boats upstream against the current but these men were considered experts.

Fly fishermen, many from the south and the Detroit area, resorted at Charlevoix, Petoskey, Walloon Lake and Harbor Springs and would arrive in East Jordan by boat or train. Sometimes the yacht Sylvia would sail down the South Arm from Charlevoix to dock at East Jordan with a fly fishing party.

Boats and gear would often be hauled up the river by horse and wagon. Even in the 1920s when trucks became available, horses were still better suited to the job since roads provided poor access. Guides would be required to get customers and as many as 30 canoes upriver as far as the old railroad bridge below Chestonia.

Two johnboats would be included to carry food and dry clothing. The parties would canoe back to town, viewing such wildflowers as orchids, tiger lilies and violets mixed among the evergreens along the way. Wild game was frequently seen including fox, mink, otter, beaver and deer. One interesting battle to watch each year was that pitting the swiftness of the river against the engineering skills of the beaver. Eventually, the beaver would always be relegated to a spot off the main stream.

Teddy Kotowich started guiding on the river in 1928. He had many prominent customers such as George Schwab and J.J. Gray of Nashville, Tenn. and later Michigan Governors Comstock and Fitzgerald, World War II General Mark Clark, Edwin J. Anderson and Buddy Parker of the Detroit Lions, Walter Buhl Ford, Julius Gilbert and many others. Many stayed at the Belvedere and Chicago Clubs of Charlevoix, Roaring Brook in Harbor Springs and the Jordan Inn.

The fishermen would always look forward to a fish dinner cooked at an isolated spot along the river. This necessitated bringing along a cooking outfit with grill, plates, silverware, bacon for cooking with the fish and other staples.

In later years the Grand Rapids Chamber of Commerce, while on their annual sail around the Great Lakes, would reserve 10 to 12 boats and guides. The guides would meet them in Harbor Springs, drive them back to East Jordan and then upriver to Graves Crossing or Chestonia Bridge to embark on a day's fishing. At the end of the trip, guides would drive them back to their boat which had spent the day sailing to Charlevoix or Traverse City. Guides who worked with Teddy included John Kotowich, Andy Anderson, Charlie Strehl, Cy Dolezel, Joe and Pete Hammond, Vern Whiteford, Keith Annear, Walter Midener, Chick DeForest, Bruce Woodcock, Bill Simmons, Al Dougherty, Bud Brown, Dallas Yettaw, Al Walden, Sarkis Sarkisian and Frank Strehl.

As more roads were developed, cars became the way of life. The fish hatchery was built with many trout ponds and the natural brook trout fishing in the river declined. Canoeing became more popular and fishermen found other forms of recreation. In 1978, after more than 50 years on the Jordan River, the "Old Fly Fisherman" Teddy Kotowich retired as a guide, and thus brought to an end a memorable era.

How the "Signature Quilt" helped build a church

BY PEGGY LOVEDAY MCKENZIE MIDENER

This close-up of the "Signature Quilt" shows the stitched signatures of contributors and the cross pattern used in the design. *Photo courtesy of Peggy Loveday McKenzie Midener.*

In East Jordan's early years, church life brought people together in many ways and helped shape the community. This story is one example. It begins with the following journal entry:

"On the 12th day of January, in the year of our Lord 1887, the ladies, whose names shall be hereafter annexed, met at the residence of Mrs. D.C. Loveday to form a Ladies Society for the purpose of doing all they possibly can to build up a protestant Episcopal Church in East Jordan."

For ten years the journal records the ladies' valiant efforts to raise money to build a church, furnish it and finally help pay off the debt. Teas, ice cream socials, excursions, musicals, sales on group-made aprons (a popular item), braided rag rugs and the very special auction of quilts made especially for the occasion brought in the largest contributions.

Of course, the five cent weekly dues slowly added up and the one dollar fee entitling gentlemen to become honorable members contributed greatly to the total, which averaged around $40 every three or four months. Fortunately, a dollar bought a lot in those days. The cornerstone was laid in August, 1989 and the church was in use by 1890.

A most ambitious project, the "Signature Quilt" was begun during the winter of 1887, with the ladies carefully stitching the names of donors in bright "turkey red" thread upon white squares. The charge was 15 cents to 25 cents per name with some businesses paying as much as 75 cents for a larger space.

It took two years to complete the quilt which seems reasonable given the fact that weekly meetings were poorly attended and the work fell largely to three or four of the faithful members. When the quilt was finally done it contained 183 names and businesses neatly arranged in blocks separated by dividers of red fabric. It was bound in red trim and made a very handsome appearance.

The auction for the quilt was held in February, 1889 at the conclusion of a fund raising dinner. The menu was a favorite: "Oysters, meats of various kinds, pies, cakes, biscuits, pickles and such articles as would garnish a table." The proceeds were $12.75 with some 30 people attending.

The beautiful Signature Quilt went to the highest bidder—my great-grandfather, D.C. Loveday—for the magnificent sum of three dollars and that is how the quilt came to be in the possession of our family.

It is still treasured by all of us and is registered and documented with Michigan State University.

Gidley's Drugstore was a traditional pharmacy

BY EVELYN GIDLEY

Gidley's Drugstore was started by James Gidley around 1900. The building was located at 101 East Main Street where a service station was later. There are a number of prescription bottles in collections with James Gidley's signature in raised letters on the glass.

During the 1917 flu epidemic, Gidley formed a partnership with Charles McNamara as a pharmacist must always be on duty in a drug store. The business was relocated to the corner of Main and Esterly and was called Gidley and Mac.

In 1923 they bought a store in Grayling and "Mac" McNamara moved there to run it. This new store was called Mac and Gidley but the East Jordan store kept the original name. The partnership continued until 1945 when it was dissolved. James Gidley's son Hugh became partner with his dad in what then became Gidley's Drugstore at the same location.

For many years the store had a soda fountain and ice cream was made by the Gidley family. They bought cream from the local dairy farmers, cut ice in winter, stored the ice during the summer and hired many local men to help freeze the ice cream at the Gidley home on Echo Street.

In 1930 they bought a counter freezer and made ice cream in the East Jordan store. There was enough to stock the store in Grayling as well. People still remember that hand packed ice cream, it tasted so good.

This photo of Gidley's Drugstore taken in the early 1920s shows the shelves packed with every pharmaceutical necessity of the time. *Photo from the collection of George Secord.*

In 1940 the marble soda fountain was taken out and the freezer was removed. The fountain was remodeled and prepackaged ice cream was purchased from Swift & Co. It was much easier to handle. Many East Jordan young people worked at the soda fountain, including the three Gidley kids.

In 1956 the store was remodeled and the soda fountain removed. It was sad to see it go, but packaged ice cream was sold everywhere and sodas, sundaes and cones were not worth the effort.

In 1978 the store became the Jordan Valley Pharmacy when Hugh sold it to his employee, Duane Chappuies, who runs it to this day.

The Temple Theatre:
Showplace of the North

BY JEAN PARDEE

It was called the "Showplace of the North" and indeed it was in its day. I'm speaking of the famous Temple Theatre which was located at 206 Main Street in East Jordan. It was there that I went to work as cashier on my 16th birthday, my first adult job. How excited I was!

As a youngster, I walked a mile and a half to town to sit in the first row, resting my feet on the front railing to marvel at Roy Rogers and Gene Autry. As I got older, I moved up into the balcony which we regarded as "some kind of heaven." Not only did I watch the love scenes on the big screen, but also kept an eye on the man who ran the projector, Roland DesJardins, who always brought his girl friend with him. Their attention to each other was hard not to notice.

Mac McDaniels was my boss and the owner of the theatre for many years. Prior to Mac's time, Hollis Drew was the owner for a very successful stint. The Theatre was built by Harry Price in 1911 shortly after an earlier theatre at the same site had been demolished.

The new Temple Theatre was renowned for its being a "first class" theatre. The Temple boasted a full, rigged stage on which many a road show appeared, as well as the finest motion pictures. In the early days, silent pictures were shown with a musical accompaniment. The first movies were in black and white; then came color and even 3-D movies.

The Temple Theatre was famed throughout Northern Michigan not only for it's state-of-the-art equipment but also it's facade which included a dazzling display of lighting. A 50-foot long "T E M P L E" sign was installed

In the 1950s, the Temple Theatre in East Jordan attracted huge crowds to first run movies, thus earning its title "Showplace of the North." *Photo from the collection of William Huckle.*

on the roof featuring six-foot high, neon letters that provided a landmark not only for boats on the lake but also planes flying at night. The Temple building also housed two businesses on either side, a cafe and an appliance merchant. The second floor of the theatre was a huge ballroom. It was wonderful!

While I was working at the theatre, Mac McDaniels choreographed several promotions, including a pretty baby contest and several talent shows. The talent show is what brought the Bundy Mountain Jamboree to town. The Bundys were a country and western band that gained community acceptance and began playing for dances in the area. Some of the members wound up making the area their home.

Mac saw the potential and opened the Temple ballroom for country dancing. This was to be the Temple's last hurrah as television was then being introduced to the area. It was the beginning of the TV craze that dropped the theatre curtains for good.

After the Temple closed the building was sold to Ben Schenck, a local realtor. Shortly thereafter it burned to the ground. There is now a parking lot where the theatre once stood.

I'm glad I wasn't around to see it go; I know a tear would have been shed since the theatre played a major role in my life. What would we do without those childhood memories we cherish so dearly?

Agnes Hegerberg's memories of old East Jordan

BY RAY KILLINGER

Agnes Hegerberg, born in 1898, remembers that growing up on East Jordan's west side was tough. She went to the Westside School located on the corner of M-66 and M-32 where a service station is today.

She remembers when the west side was the only side. The bridge had not yet been built and the east side was just hills. The foundry had not been built. Soon, activity and interest began to bubble for the east side of the lake. A boat service from Charlevoix began. The boat was the Hum with Captain Jepson at the helm. He landed regularly at an area that is now just to the west of the bridge. This boat service went both to and from Charlevoix and also acted as a ferry to the east side.

The building of the bridge indeed changed things. The foundry was completed and another downtown was forming, much larger than the west side downtown area. Soon, many businesses flourished, including two banks: State Bank and Peoples Bank. Agnes worked for Peoples bank for a while and indicated that she felt Peoples was a more popular bank, but less important.

This bank was housed in the building that The EJ Shop is now located in. The second bank in town at that time, State Bank, was located on the corner of Main and Esterly, where the Main Street Hair Cottage now resides. Agnes' most memorable person connected to these banks was a fellow who lived in the country surrounding East Jordan. Seems this fellow took out a note with the bank, borrowing the money apparently for his farm. The funny part seems to be that this person was seen returning to the bank regularly to renew his loan. It appeared that he never paid it in full, and that it seemed okay with him in that it cost him a mere 50 cents to renew the note each time. Agnes indicated that the man was still coming to the bank even after she stopped working there!

Back then the banks sold many products that were not really bank products, such as insurance, in a shop within the bank. Also, the bank handled many farming matters in a side office. Few people really knew or understood what went on in those side offices, but the customers seemed to go in and come out happy!

There were few bank robberies in those days. Apparently people worked so hard that they didn't have the strength to consider a robbery. One did happen, however, in Bellaire and word of the robbery got out that the robbers were headed straight for East Jordan to pull off another job. The days came and went and the robbers weren't caught, nor did they ever show up in East Jordan.

As the town grew, Agnes remembers how Main Street looked. Sherman's Hardware Store, was next to a baked goods store (the present-day City Building). Agnes had the good fortune to have spent a little time living above it and still recalls all those heavenly aromas coming from the store each day. Agnes talks of Main Street, with its dime stores, gas stations and theaters, just like she were still there. The glimmer in her eyes tells that it was indeed a special time of life for her.

Alexander Bush: Portrait of a Union soldier

BY GEOFFREY D. REYNOLDS

Alexander Bush and business partner F.L. Wilson moved to East Jordan in 1886 to open a barrel hoop mill. Wilson was the inventor of a new type of barrel hoop and the two had previously operated a hoop mill in West Bay City. They were drawn to East Jordan by an abundance of elm wood in the area.

While Bush went on to become a very successful businessman in the East Jordan/Lake Charlevoix area, his more significant place in local history is as one of East Jordan's longest surviving Civil War veterans—and a distinguished one at that.

The adventurous and heroic Bush began his life in Chapin's Corners near Hopewell, Ontario County, New York on November 8, 1837. He was one of eleven children of Andrew M. and Jane Bush. His father died when Bush was 12. At 16 Bush became a brakeman on the New York Central railway.

Along with his sister Evelyn he traveled by ship to San Francisco in 1854 and became a gold miner, but was only mildly successful. After four years he returned to New York State and then traveled to Michigan in 1859 to live with two of his brothers. They settled near Ann Arbor where he met and married Miss Jennie McCormick.

On July 15, 1862 Gov. Austin Blair made a plea for volunteers to help fill the call by President Abraham Lincoln for 300,000 more men. On August 11, 1862, after the United States had been engulfed in a civil war for more than a year, Alexander Bush, at five feet, ten inches in height and weighing 150 pounds, left the little town of Superior and joined the 20th Michigan Infantry, Company F at Salem, Michigan. Seven days later he was mustered in at Jackson and the regiment left for Washington, D.C. on September 1, 1862.

He enlisted as a corporal but was quickly upgraded to a sergeant and then color sergeant. He carried the colors at Fredricksburg, Knoxville, Louden and Vicksburg before returning to the Army of the Potomac, then at the battles of Wilderness, Spotsylvania and Cold Harbor.

On July 30, 1864, after spending nine months in the trenches near Petersburg, Virginia, the 20th was ordered to charge toward a recently exploded mine known as the "Crater." They charged through an open field and lost about half the charging men to the crossfire from rebel forces.

The commanding officer, a Col. Cutcheon, filed this report: "We charged at 8 a.m. in the face of terrific fire of musketry, canister and shell and maintained our position, efficiently assisting in repulsing three assaults until 7:30 p.m., losing 52 out of 110 men. After that ill-fated day we remembered with some pride and consolation that ours were the last Union colors displayed from the enemy's works."

Bush had been carrying those colors. With only about 20 of his compatriots left and the enemy mounting a final charge, Bush helped to cut up the colors and bury them in the sand before being taken prisoner by the rebel forces.

Bush later recalled the incident for a New York newspaper which ran this account: "Naturally the firing was pretty hot in the neighborhood of the colors and some of the boys were anxious that he (Bush) carry the flag to the rear, but this he declined to do because he wanted the troops behind to know they were still holding the fort. He planted the flag upon the breastworks and was making good use of a musket when a piece from a shell shattered the shaft and the colors went down for the first time. Soon a white flag was raised and with others to the tune of about 600, he was taken prisoner and confined at Danville."

Bush was lucky to survive a five-month stay at Danville Prison; of the 7,500 prisoners held, 1,141 died, mostly of smallpox which ravaged the town in December, 1863. He was eventually released and was sent to Richmond and later Varina, Virginia where he was paroled on October 17, 1864.

The following December 21, Bush was sent to Detroit, where at Michigan's newly built Harper Hospital barracks for Civil War soldiers, he hoped to recover from conditions suffered while in prison.

In this photo taken in his later years, Alexander Bush is shown on the left with W.P. Porter standing and another unidentified gentleman on the right. *Photo from the Portside Art and Historical Museum collection.*

Bush spent two weeks convalescing from "chronic rheumatism" as Patient No. 879.

After a seven-day furlough at his home near Ann Arbor, Bush returned to active duty at Petersburg, Virginia, where he had last served before being captured. He accepted a promotion to First Lieutenant in Company G of the 20th Michigan and later rose to Captain. On May 30, 1865 he was honorably discharged.

After the end of hostilities Bush began a washboard manufacturing firm in Mason, Michigan. He left Mason for Saginaw in 1879 and in 1882 moved to West Bay City where he and Wilson opened their first hoop mill. After selling the washboard factory in 1886 Bush and Wilson moved north to East Jordan to open their new mill.

They operated the mill on the west side of town until the elm supply was exhausted in 1892. While in East Jordan Bush helped organize the local Grand Army of the Republic (GAR) Stevens Post #66.

Soon after the closing of the hoop mill, Bush and Reuben Glenn bought East Jordan's only bank. Bush later sold his interest in the bank in 1896 and began buying and selling timberland until 1901. He built a saw mill on Lake Charlevoix which burned in January of 1902. In 1904 Bush's first wife died. He later married Dora Timmerman who died in 1923.

Alexander Bush died in 1933 at the age of 95, East Jordan's last Grand Army veteran and member of the Rebec-Sweet Post. His body is interred at the Maple Grove Cemetery in Mason, Michigan.

Early Christmas traditions

BY JODY MALPASS CLARK

In East Jordan's early years, the community had a rich mix of European immigrant families. At Christmas time, each ethnic group's celebration would incorporate traditions from the Old Country.

Frank Kubicek's parents came to the Bohemian Settlement from Bohemia when he was 14 months old. One year his Christmas tree was decorated with doughnuts, but they didn't last long with a naughty little boy in the house. He remembers his father singing Czech Christmas songs with fervor.

St. John Nepomucene Catholic Church, built by the Bohemian settlers, would smell of evergreen at Christmas time because all the heating stoves would be going.

Ralph Josifek, who lives on a Michigan centennial farm in the settlement, recalled that the children gave recitations in the Czech language. St. Nikolas was not always giving; only if a child was good would there be fruit, candy, practical home made gifts or, sometimes, a little toy.

One year Ralph's mother scrimped all summer to buy him a tin peacock that he wound up to squeak and walk along the floor. "We were very careful with our toys," he said, "because we knew there would be no more if we broke them."

They were served chicken, homemade noodles, wheat and poppy seed rolls filled with prune or cheese, and vanocka, a plaited raisin bread.

The German Settlement

The face of this little East Jordan girl—or is it a boy?—on Christmas morning, says everything about the joy of finding just what you wanted under the tree. *Photo from the collection of William Huckle.*

feasted on their own smoked ham and perhaps a duck, with stollen and cookies according to Emma Walters. People came to the Lutheran Church by sleigh from as far as ten miles away.

"They were all half frozen by the time they got there," recalled Emma. "Then they had to find a place for their horses."

Most of the gifts had to be practical. Said Emma, "I once got a doll with a glass head. Other than that, I had very, very few toys."

Frank Behling remembers it as the only time they could afford cookies and cake, candy and nuts. "Sometimes there was a pair of socks, new britches, a handmade sled or skies made of barrel stays," he said.

In Little Norway the tree was decorated with glass beads, carved pails and utensils and blown glass birds with tinsel wings. Marie Hughes remembers the neighbors coming to hold hands and sing Norwegian carols. When the tree was lit her father would be nearby with a pole and wet rags in case something caught fire. Dinner was smoked fish, bread, rich rice pudding and cookies.

Irish Immigrants would also give practical gifts with family visits. Archie Murphy's mother would knit stockings, mittens and caps for her 12 children. The Grange was the center for social life.

The Polish settlers' Christmas celebration centered around St. Augustus Catholic

This 1888 holiday choir included some well known East Jordan residents. From the left are Frank Kenyon, W.P. Porter, a Mrs. Smith, Mrs. Kenyon, Estella Sherman, W.E. Malpass and organist Mamie Stone. *Photo from the Portside Art and Historical Museum collection.*

Church in Boyne Falls. On Christmas Eve they would have pork, braided breads and plum pudding. "Dad would go down and buy a local newspaper, then tear it in thin strips to trim the tree," according to Victoria Kosc. There would be straw on the floor for the children to roll in which was removed on New Year's Day leaving hardwood floors that shone as if they had been waxed.

For English Christmas dinner, families had plum pudding which would typically make a grand entrance to the table. In the William and Alice Malpass household, Mother and her 13 children made many gifts. Recalls Alice Malpass Nesman, one of the 13, "It was fun to see what all the whispered conferences were about."

"People were paid less, things cost less, people bought less, they needed less," she noted. "My brothers Richard and Ted had skis, but they had to make their own. They soaked the point ends of lumber in the big reservoir of the kitchen range to turn them up, hammered leather straps across the middles, then skied down Water Tower Hill."

The Ladies Aid sewed innumerable small tartan stockings to fill with candy. Santa came at the end of the service at the church, which was always packed on Christmas Eve. There was a rustling and turning of heads, watching as the back door opened and a fat, red-suited Santa would distribute the stockings. "Silent Night" was sung as families returned home. 🌿

W.P. Porter and the East Jordan Lumber Company

BY GRACE GALMORE

William Pitt Porter was born in Butler County, Pennsylvania on October 4, 1853. He came with his father, John Porter, to Leelanau County in 1855. He was only two years old at this time.

John Porter came to the region to do missionary work among the Indians and in the school which he established there. William soon learned to speak the Indian tongue. There were four more children born to the family: three girls, Carie, Agnes and Harriet, and one boy, Frank.

As he grew older, William received training at the Indian School but later became determined to secure a college education. With this aim in mind he sent to the nearest college for the preparatory course which was required. Working days and nights he mastered the course and was about ready to go to school when his father suddenly decided that he and his wife would spend the winter in their old home state of Pennsylvania.

Being the oldest child, William had to give up any further thought of going to college. Instead he took on the responsibility of looking after the other Porter children which was quite a task as Frank was very young at the time.

At the age of 26, William's ambition turned to a different pursuit. Having become interested in the great lumbering opportunities emerging in northern Michigan, he moved to East Jordan to become a partner with his uncle Joseph C. Glenn in a sawmill. This was the mill known as "Mill A." The timber in the immediate region was all hardwood, the pine forests being further inland.

The Glenn and Porter Mill had a capacity of 25,000 feet of lumber per day and initially employed 12 men.

A second mill known as "Mill B" or the "Red Mill" was built by a man named Stoepel and Joseph Martin.

W.P. Porter's portrait still hangs in the board room of the bank he helped found. *Photo courtesy of FMB Bank.*

It became the Stoepel Lumber Co. but after changing hands about seven times was bought in a sheriff's sale by Porter.

Glenn sold his interest in Mill A to Porter and the latter entered into a partnership with Ames and Frost, a bicycle manufacturing firm in Chicago. The operation eventually became the East Jordan Lumber

The Glenn & Porter Mill, which became the East Jordan Lumber Company's Mill A, could process 25,000 board feet of lumber a day. *Photo from the collection of William Huckle.*

Company with W.P. Porter as president. The land holdings of this company expanded until they included a very considerable amount of real estate and industries in and around East Jordan.

By January, 1894 the company was advertising for as many as 50 teams to haul logs. According to a December 12, 1894 newspaper account, "Mr. L.A. Hoyt, lumber inspector, reports that during the past season which has been very light, there were 141 vessels loaded at our docks, outside the regular lines of boats. The first arrival was April 6 and the last appearance November 29. There was shipped, in round numbers, 15 million feet of lumber, 6,000 cords of wood, 6,000 cords of bark and 3,000 ties and posts. This is equal to 3,000 carloads of freight from this place alone and does not include the brick which is manufactured here."

At the peak of the lumber boom, W.P. Porter was the largest employer in the region with about 500 on the payroll. A large general store was operated by the East Jordan Lumber Company as an accommodation to its employees. Everything from meats to clothing was carried in stock. At its peak the store did

over $1 million a year in business.

In July, 1901 the East Jordan & Southern Railroad was incorporated. This was owned by the East Jordan Lumber Company and at one time had 55 miles of trackage. The first locomotive was one that had been used on the Chicago Elevated Railways before that system was changed to electric. It was called a "dinky" as it was so small.

The locomotive was brought to East Jordan on a barge in 1899 and greatly taxed the ingenuity of the owners in getting it unloaded. It was brought to the place where the East Jordan city marina now stands and almost caused the sinking of the vessel on which it rode when it was drawn to shore across heavy-planking laid from the shore to the side of the boat.

In a report of the State Tax Commission on valuation of Michigan railroads in January 1904, the East Jordan & Southern was shown going from $120,000 to $160,000 that year. By 1912 it was assessed at $235,000.

In 1903 another new industry was formed in East Jordan, the Pine Lake Flooring Company. It had an initial capitalization of $40,000, most of which was subscribed by local residents. W.P. Porter was named

These employees of the East Jordan Lumber Company Store, (from left) Will Hawkins, Walter Johnson and Ervin Hiatt, were photographed in 1916 cutting up a 500-pound wheel of Monarch cheese at 2 a.m., probably to get portions ready for business the next day. *Photo from the collection of George Secord.*

president. Plans were for a first-class maple flooring plant with capacity to make 25,000 feet of flooring per day and a total employment of 75 men.

The flooring manufactured at this plant did indeed prove to be some of the best in the world. W.E. Malpass, founder of the East Jordan Iron Works and a close friend of W.P. Porter, traveled back to his native England in 1897 and while in London secured a market for the maple flooring for as long as the supply lasted. They considered it first class. When local supplies were used up, however, the Pine Lake Flooring Co. switched to maple from the Upper Peninsula. This was rejected by the English buyers as not up to grade and that was the end of the deal.

W.P. Porter not only built a successful business but took on civic responsibility and tried in every way to improve conditions in the town. He served as village president and when East Jordan was incorporated as a city in 1911, the chartering documents bear his signature as alderman. He served for many years on the school board and was president or director of the State Bank most of his later life.

Porter and his wife, the former Harriet Jamison of Butler County, Pennsylvania raised a family of three girls: Mary, Flora and Esther, and three boys: John, Howard and Donald.

He was a charter member of the Presbyterian Church, sang in the choir, taught Sunday School and was an elder for many years. His was a kind, tactful unassuming personality. He shunned publicity, preferring to work through other people whenever possible. He financed the work of a missionary, Dr. C.R. Harper in Brazil, established a scholarship at the East Jordan High School and supported a summer program at the Presbyterian Church that brought many nationally famous ministers to the church to preach.

All was not smooth sailing for Porter; he experienced some setbacks in his life. One was the boiler explosion at the Red Mill in 1892 that killed eight workers. He suffered a broken leg once when a small railroad handcar on which he was riding jumped the track as it was being run off on a siding at the approach of a train. Later in life, Porter suffered from rheumatism and had to go away for treatment.

These things probably made him more conscious of others' suffering, as he was always aiding those who needed help. When his hearing became impaired in his later years, he had a special acoustic system installed in the church so others similarly afflicted might enjoy the service.

W.P. Porter died in 1939 at the age of 86, having lived a full life. East Jordan owes much to this man; there are few lives here that have not been affected by his influence.

Rockery School was a typical one-room school

BY FERN L. MORRIS

The area where the Rockery School began was not inhabited by white settlers until after the Civil War when the government was giving any interested Union veteran 40 acres in northern Michigan. During this period, in the early 1870s, it was not unusual to have Indian trails winding through the settlers' homesteads.

In the early 1880s a school was established in Section 27 just off of what is now Morris Road. My great grandfather Williams went to that first Rockery School. Only a small clearing remains today where that school stood. In the 1890s—1894 I believe—a regular schoolhouse was built in Section 23 and the building is still there. All the lumber for the structure was hauled from Elmira, as was lumber for many houses in the vicinity.

By the turn of the century, the area was populated by such names as Blanchard, Blaha, Caukin, Williams, Kowalski, Sleeper, Pinney, Ellis, Sweet, Brewer, Sonnabend, Nemecec, Thompson, White, Skrocki, Jones, Krol, Valencourt and Sommerville among others.

In 1907 the teacher at Rockery School was Ethel Fish. Miss Fish was paid $22.50 twice a month plus $2 a month for doing her own janitor work. That work, incidentally, included not only sweeping and dusting, but also building a fire in the heating stove and making sure the one-room school was warm when the children arrived in the morning.

And what an experience it must have been when they arrived! The group would have included anywhere from 15 to 35 students, ranging in age from five to 15 years old and studying at levels from kindergarten to eighth grade. There would usually be at least

Classes at the Rockery School's one-room schoolhouse probably looked very much like this group of students who posed in the early 1900s at the Cedar Valley School. *Photo from the collection of Frances Edwards.*

one child from a recent immigrant family who spoke no English. This meant the teacher had to teach English to a child, with no training or knowledge of the child's first language which at the time was typically Polish or German.

Leaphy Schooly took over as teacher in 1909 for $40 a month. To put the value of a dollar at the time into perspective, that same year the school bought 21 cords of hardwood, cut, split, delivered and stacked for $1.90 a cord, $2 a cord for kindling.

In 1912 Arloene Jones, my great aunt, became the teacher and stayed until 1920. Then came Prudy Caukin who had been teaching at Mt. Bliss. She lived across the road from Rockery School and taught until she became totally disabled by rheumatoid arthritis in 1940.

One aspect of one-room schools that provides food for thought today is how they handled what we call special education. Those dedicated teachers, realizing the special needs and limitations of some of their students, taught them to the extent that they had the ability to learn without making them feel inferior or superior.

Prudy Caukin was a master at that. When I started at Rockery School in April of my third grade year, I did not know my multiplication tables. Miss Caukin made me use half of my lunch hour to work with her to learn them and catch up with the rest of the class. I now realize that she had given up half of her lunch hour, too.

After Prudy left, the Rockery School had a progression of five teachers, Ella Gilkerson, Mabel Liberty, Ralph Josifek, my mother Rena Morris and Anna Payne, who each taught one year. Unable to find a teacher in 1946, the school began transporting students to East Jordan. Since the East Jordan bus went only to the district line, all the Rockery students had to gather to meet it at the intersection of Old State and Williams Road.

Four years later the decision was made to consolidate and Rockery School ceased to exist. Although it officially became part of the East Jordan Consolidated School District in 1950, that one-room school is still very real in the hearts and minds of all who attended it. 🦢

Close call on the "bob"

BY JODY MALPASS CLARK

There have been numerous references within my family to the fun they used to have on bobsleds many years ago. While going through my parents photos I found one of the 12-man bob that figures in the following story, told by my father, R.W. Malpass, engineer and past Chairman of the Board for the East Jordan Iron Works.

"We used to position someone at the bottom of the hill on Main Street to watch for oncoming traffic. One time the lookout must have been daydreaming because it was after the bob had already gotten started that he started waving frantically. But we had gotten up too much steam to stop.

"We tried to swerve and there were people falling off left and right but the bob hit the flat, ran between the legs of a horse drawing a sled and continued down

The 12-man bobsled, shown here poised at 105 Garfield for a run down toward the lake, provided many days of winter fun in East Jordan. *Photo from the collection of Jody Malpass Clark.*

the hill to the lake. The horse fell, splat. Once again, we were hauled up the hill and reported to our mother. That man was angry!" 🦢

Early tourism:
Ed's Boats and Cottages

BY ADELINE BOWERMAN

The story of "Ed's Boats" started in 1938 (or '39) when Keith Dressel sold Edgar Bowerman 220 feet of Lake Charlevoix shoreline along with a piece of property directly across M-66 on Lord Road. Later, he bought an adjoining property from the Alice Clink estate and the Earl Clark lot on the lake.

While still living and working downstate, Ed built nine row boats and brought them to East Jordan with the hopes of establishing a marina and selling bait to fishermen. To rent the boats, however, he needed tourists.

Since there were very few rental cabins for vacationers, he decided to build three one-bedroom log cottages. The cottages were built by local men using logs from the Frank Severance farm. Ed and his friends, Frank Stucker and Woody Anderson, came up from their work in Detroit on weekends to supervise the building project.

By the summer of 1940 "Ed's Boats and Cottages" was ready for business. He employed his father and mother as caretakers while he continued working at Hudson Motor.

In the summer of 1942, Ed invited me to go with him to East Jordan to meet his parents and see his business. He took me for a canoe ride down the Jordan River from Graves Crossing. I was sold on the area and we were married the following December.

At the end of World War II in August, 1945, we brought our belongings and our four and a half month old son, Donald, north to make East Jordan our home and take care of Ed's Boats and Cottages. We bought a 10 by 16 foot building from Ed Portz and had it moved to the business location so it could be our office and

summer "home." We moved into one of the cottages for the winter.

In 1946 we built our log home and moved the marina business into the basement. Two years later, we put two two-bedroom cottages on the Clark lot. That fall, Mr. Wade hired me to teach a first and second grade "overflow" room at the East Jordan Elementary School.

As the tourist industry grew, so did we. In 1953 we had the Swan Motel built on the Clink property. The next summer we sold the Marina and three cabins to Charles and Ilah Richter who changed the name to Ric's Boats. While we operated Ed's Boats and Cottages, we made many friends, a number of whom returned to the East Jordan area to buy property and establish homes.

TOP: Young Donald Bowerman is shown shortly after the family moved north to East Jordan. BOTTOM: This is a view of Ed's Cottages from the water. *Photos courtesy of Adeline Bowerman.*

My grandfather the railroad engineer

BY JOHN BRENNAN

My maternal grandfather, Art Farmer, was a well known railroad engineer in East Jordan for many years. He started working for what would become known as the East Jordan and Southern Railroad at an early age, somewhere around 16 or 17 years old, and retired from the EJ&S in 1946.

The story I was told was that Mr. Porter, owner of the East Jordan Lumber Co., observed him splicing a steel cable at one of their log loading sites and decided they could use him in the logging network.

Much of his education in steam engineering came from on-the-job training. Art could and did dismantle locomotives and put them together again. Being a small man, about 5'1", it was amazing to see him and one other man put locomotive No. 6 back on the track when it became derailed at the Esterly St. crossing near the old city pier.

I was about nine years old when he spotted me watching the process. He came over and asked me to leave because there would probably be some language that he was sure my mother wouldn't want me to hear.

Another "Art story" involves a train mishap. On Saturdays the logging railroad transported lumberjacks to town for their recreation. There was also a regular passenger run to Bellaire that connected with the Pere Marquette Railroad. Somehow, both trains were on the same track going opposite directions and they bumped. The irony is that Art was the engineer on one train and his younger brother Earl was the engineer on the other. This was one incident that, you could say, was "all in the family."

Art normally got up at 4 a.m. and had a good breakfast; his wife, my Grandma Stella, was a very good

In this 1909 photo of East Jordan & Southern locomotive No. 5, Art Farmer is seated at the far right. Others include, top row left to right, George Ramsey, James Howard and Judson Wing. In the bottom row are William Rains, Earle B. Farmer and Marshall Barnette. *Photo from the collection of Virginia Kaake-Giacomelli.*

cook. He went out the door dressed in heavy black pants and jacket, wearing his distinctive hat with tasseled top, short beak and flaps that could be put down over his ears. His foot gear consisted of laced felt boots with rubber slip-ons.

Sunday, however, was the day of the suit. For Art, that was quite a transformation from his work day clothes. Even though he was not in the choir, Art enjoyed singing in a clear tenor voice at church...and about anywhere else. "Silver threads amongst the gold" and a rather long song called "I was born ten thousand years ago an' I can lick the man who sez it isn't so!" were favorites.

On the job, Art was a memorable worker. One of the times that Howard and Maude Porter, major stock holders of the railroad, were returning to East Jordan on the train, it stopped in the middle of nowhere. Maude asked Howard about the unscheduled stop, to which he replied, "I think Art spotted some flowers to take home to his Stella."

From farm fields to fairways: the story of Ammon Beers

BY BARBARA ADAMS

One hundred and thirty years ago, who would have dreamed that land cleared and farmed by a new young homesteader would someday become a playground for local residents and visitors?

In 1865, 19-year old Ammon Beers moved from Charlevoix to settle on the property on Ferry Road now known as Ye Nyne Old Holles Golf Club. This beautiful piece of property, overlooking Lake Charlevoix and a Chippewa village, was much like home to Ammon. He had spent his early years in Northport, Michigan as one of only two white children in a school comprised primarily of Indian children. He thus felt right at home among the Chippewas.

Ammon received the first piece of this property in the form of an 1865 land grant signed by President Andrew Johnson. A second portion was also obtained through a land grant, this one authorized in 1870 by President Ulysses S. Grant.

In 1869 Ammon married Jennie Black, a young lady from Charlevoix. They raised four daughters. Ammon and Jennie cleared the land and farmed just enough to feed their family and sell a small surplus to buy staples. Ammon owned schooners and engaged in fishing for several years. He also carried passengers and freight to several different points on Lake Michigan.

He later worked as a clerk in the store of William Lister of Charlevoix.

Ammon and Jenny Beers are shown here in their 80s. Their daughter Eva always bought their clothes and, even in their later years, bought them a couple sizes larger than necessary in case they grew. *Photo courtesy of Barbara Adams.*

Ammon would skate to Charlevoix in the winter to get supplies. Sometimes he would take a team of horses and bring home such necessities as molasses, sugar, flour and coffee, and also some treats such as licorice and horehound.

The only road was a trail through the woods so he would leave at four in the morning and be gone all day. In the warm season he would sometimes row his boat three and a half miles across the lake to Horton Bay to trade with Captain Carlo, but most of his supplies were bought in Charlevoix, his old home town.

During the time Ammon and Jennie lived on the property, they had many Chippewa visitors and neighbors. Family members recall stories of bartering with the Indians. One Chippewa neighbor named Nockwan lived at the back of the property toward Loomis Road. From his tree house he would watch to see where the chickens laid their eggs. He would then gather according to his needs and leave a basket or some other hand crafted item as payment.

Stories were passed down of other Chippewas in the neighborhood. Wishagesics, with his squaw and children, rolled up in blankets down by the lake. Peter Mitchell, who was known as "Old One Arm," would come and sleep on the floor of Ammon's house and be gone early the next morning. His nickname was acquired when he came home late one night, laid too close to the fire and burned his arm off. Washagua lived in a wigwam of deerskins and porcupine needles on the shores of Lake Charlevoix and ran fish nets belonging to Ammon. All these arrangements were friendly. Ammon had been raised with Chippewa Indians as a young boy and his friendship with them was strong throughout his life.

In 1923 Ammon and Jennie sold the lake view property and moved to a small stone cottage on Ridge Road that belonged to their daughter and son-in-law, Frank and Belle Wangeman. They remained there until their deaths in 1934.

Today, if you are a golfer, or you just wish to ride or walk around the Ye Nyne Old Holles golf course, stop and think back of the young Ammon Beers and his dream. Imagine the hours of labor it took to clear the land. Picture the Chippewa village and the lake shore below and appreciate the peaceful beauty that has been preserved for us to enjoy today. 🦢

The Cooperage

BY TOM BREAKEY, SR.

On September 22, 1903, people on their way to the County Fair in East Jordan saw a little office being constructed near the fairgrounds just west of the East Jordan and Southern Railroad tracks. This was to become one of the community's largest industries in the early part of the century, a facility that was known to most residents as "the Cooperage."

The plant was one of 23 factories owned by the Greif Bros. Company of Ohio, which at the time was the largest barrel-making, or cooperage, company in the world. The East Jordan factory employed at least 160 at its peak and the payroll for a fortnight amounted to $2,334 in 1904 and 1905. Machinery in the plant was valued at $10,000.

The Cooperage manufactured slack cooperage and barrel and keg stock that was marketed throughout the country. Some of its products were even shipped overseas. Its production capacity required two cars of lumber a day.

I lived directly across the East Jordan and Southern Railroad tracks from the Cooperage in the early 1920s. My recollections of it include a large, red wooden building with a cupola on the roof, partially obscured by huge decks of hemlock logs.

There was a two-story boarding house east of the railroad tracks on the north side of the street, and many company houses along the tracks north of the boarding house. More were on Cooperage Street and South Maple.

All the company houses were built from the same plans with little variation. They were approximately 26 feet square with a "hip" roof and a brick chimney in the middle. The interior was divided into a living room, dining room, two small bedrooms and a mini-kitchen. Some, but not all, sported hardwood floors and a bay window. Each back yard had an outhouse and a water pump near the back door. With no insulation and no storm windows, these houses never lacked for fresh air, both summer and winter.

The plant was destroyed by fire in 1905 and was rebuilt. In 1910 or 1911 the drying kiln burned and the mill was torn down and taken to Manistique in the Upper Peninsula.

I cannot pinpoint when the Cooperage finally ceased operation altogether, but I do remember scavengers digging up the steampipes that ran underground from building to building. The main building itself was dismantled over a period of years. Joseph Kortanek carried the lumber away on his back to his home at 113 Cooperage Street where he used it to build a barn and front porch on his house.

After the factory closed the houses were sold and moved to new locations in and around town. Those that have not been changed structurally can still be easily identified today.

Interestingly, as of 1995, Greif Bros. was still in the barrel manufacturing business in Ohio, although today the barrels are made out of paper instead of wood. 🦢

The Jordan Valley Co-Operative Creamery

BY DAVID L. KNIGHT

The Jordan Valley Cooperative Creamery was founded in the autumn of 1931 following extensive work by major dairy farmers in the Lake Charlevoix area. These producers knew they were being paid six to nine cents less per pound of butterfat than was being received by producers in central and southern Michigan.

The other contributing factor to the formation of the Creamery was a major economic depression which at the time was just beginning to get a firm grip on the nation. Farm prices were declining to the ridiculous stage and it was hard to detect whether northern Michigan herd owners were being discriminated against in the price paid for butterfat or whether business conditions were so poor it was impossible to get more money.

The first Creamery was housed in a former garage and potato warehouse. After a new building was constructed in 1949, the original Creamery became a car repair shop. *Photo from the Portside Art and Historical Museum collection.*

There was one obvious answer for the dairy herd owners: get in business for themselves and find out. A general meeting of all dairy farmers in the Lake Charlevoix area was held in East Jordan and the Jordan Valley Cooperative Creamery was founded. By early spring, 1932, sufficient stock had been subscribed to open a plant. A building committee was elected and the new industry purchased a garage building measuring 60 by 60 feet at the corner of Spring and Esterly Streets. The business, managed by Percy Penfold, opened on June 8, 1932.

Over the next 17 years, the Creamery grew from a small operation that processed 237,443 pounds of butterfat its first year to one that produced over 1.6 million pounds in 1948. Plans for a major expansion emerged in the early 1940s but were delayed by World War II, during which the government appropriated much of the plant's output. Work was finally started in August, 1946 on a new plant. Cost: $150,000. With a myriad of wartime government regulations and approvals to wade through, work was suspended that autumn and did not resume until the following March.

The facility was finally completed on February 3, 1949. The Board of Directors of the Jordan Valley Cooperative Creamery at the time included Archie Murphy and Elmer Murray of East Jordan, William Parsons and Clint Blanchard of Charlevoix, Howard Stephens of Boyne City and Edward Wiltse and G.P. VanderArk of Ellsworth. Percy Penfold continued as manager.

The Creamery operated for several more years before the declining number of dairy herds in Charlevoix and other market factors caused it to be closed. The building was eventually purchased by the East Jordan Iron Works as their corporate office and was renovated and expanded by EJIW once again in 1994-95.

The memorable Loveday Opera House

BY PEGGY LOVEDAY MCKENZIE MIDENER

The elegant Loveday Opera House, built in 1900 on the corner of Main Street and Williams, featured a wide assortment of entertainment from traveling theater companies to musical performances by local artists. *Photo from the collection of Peggy Loveday McKenzie Midener.*

At the turn of the century, an opera house was not just for singing, especially in a small village such as East Jordan.

It was a place for a great variety of entertainment. Stage plays predominated but many evenings were spent celebrating local events and hosting musical performances by talented townspeople. Dances were held at the opera house and it served as a focal point for social activities.

Long winter nights were made cheerier when one could go to a good play put on by a traveling theatre company. And audience members could look forward to actually meeting the players at a reception after the last act.

The first such facility in East Jordan was called the East Jordan Opera House and was owned and managed by W. Asa Loveday and Frank Martinek about 1895. They were charter members of the Dramatic Club and apparently put on plays of quality high enough to fill the 450 seats which were advertised as being comfortable.

Five years later, a new Opera House was built on

98

Main Street and Williams. This one seated 800 comfortably and had a 48-foot wide stage that was 27 feet deep with a 15-foot proscenium arch. It was billed as "the neatest and best equipped house outside the larger cities" and it's motto was "One night's good business is better than a dozen night's poor business (we know the town and know how many attractions can do good business per month)."

By 1904, electricity had replaced the acetylene gas lighting and innovation was on its way. This meant the earliest silent movies could be shone—and they were. The movies were often supplied with appropriate piano music by Constance Loveday, the young daughter and granddaughter of W. Asa and Douglas C. Loveday, managers and owners of the Loveday Opera House.

Excursions to the opera house were offered by train and boat for the convenience of patrons living in Charlevoix, Petoskey and all points served by the rail system. Stock companies came from New York, Chicago, New Orleans and other large theatrical centers that relied on their touring companies to cover as many towns as possible on their midwest circuits and acquaint the "rurals" with the allure of the theatre.

It was not a hard task because the audience was hungry for good entertainment and loved a melodrama as much as a "farcical comedy in good taste." Even Shakespeare's tragedies were applauded, wept over, and talked about for weeks. "Uncle Tom's Cabin," a four act play featuring A.L. Martin's Stock Co., was performed to standing room only and was held over an extra night. The October, 1906 program listed a cast of 25 actors, including several children. The program also listed such coming events as a Catholic Society Bazaar, Annual Thanksgiving Mask Ball and two more plays. It also announced the news that a new drop curtain was expected sometime during the month.

All the programs contained advertising from local businesses and often a few admonitions from the manager, such as:

"It is the policy of this theatre to present nothing but attractions of merit—the kind which will send an audience away after the final curtain feeling that they have been well repaid for their expense and time. It is his desire that the patrons in all parts of the house will take pride in encouraging the maintenance of good order.

"Applause, whenever warranted is always most thoroughly appreciated by the "stage folk" and can be fully shown by clapping of hands. Whistling and stamping of feet is strictly forbidden.

"No gentleman will soil the floor with tobacco.

"Ladies will kindly remove their hats while seated.

"Any discourtesy shown by house personnel should be reported to the manager.

"With the cooperation of the patrons, I shall endeavor to make this one of the best conducted houses in Michigan and feel sure that East Jordan will be classed as one of the towns which the best attractions will not pass by."

—W. A. Loveday, Manager

From the opening program, "A Wise Woman," August 3, 1899, in which the East Jordan Orchestra furnished selections between acts, to the final months in 1909 to 1910 when the theatre was open every evening with a "fine program of Vaudeville, motion pictures, and illustrated songs—"an effort will be made to serve the very best talent available and the latest and best films. Admission: Adults 10 cents, children 5 cents"—the manager worked hard to please and educate the growing audience.

It all came to an end April 2, 1910, when the Opera House burned to the ground in the early morning hours. There is a little park there now—the G.A.R. park, the land having been sold to the city for the sum of one dollar for that purpose.

The playbills, letter heads from stock companies and most of the programs are among the many historical odd and ends treasured by the W. Asa Loveday descendants. They suggest so many stories and leave so many questions unanswered.

The Wagbo farm and Norwegian settlement

BY RICK MEISTERHEIM

In mid-19th century Norway there was much talk of the lumbering and farming which could be done in Michigan. Many young men and women without a way to gain land or money for themselves set out for the United States, having learned of the opportunities there from friends and relatives who had already emigrated.

The first Norwegian to settle in East Jordan was Henry Waagbo. Before coming to East Jordan, Waagbo lived in Northport where he logged with a crew. He married a French woman who never was welcomed by his Norse friends and relatives and had two girls. Henry's wife became discouraged at the hospitality accorded her and left her husband and the two children.

Waagbo had quite a struggle caring for these two small girls and working. He left Northport and came to East Jordan. The story is told how he carried one child on his back while he held the hand of the other and went from place to place seeking a home for the little ones and himself. Finally he found places with two different families for the children (who later adopted them).

Waagbo then homesteaded an 80-acre piece of land, on which he built a home. He married a woman of his own nationality and they proceeded to live there. The new wife was not happy in this pioneering and wanted to move back to her home town of Suttons Bay. She finally persuaded him to sell the property to an enterprising relative, Ole Waagbo.

The deal was made in cash and the deed signed over to the new owner. Henry was so distraught over leaving his farm that he decided to pay the money back and get his land back. When he went to look for the suitcase in which he had put the money, it was gone. Actually his wife had taken it for safer keeping, but he did not know that. In his great sorrow over the whole business of first losing his home and then the money, he went out to the barn and hung himself.

That farm, about three miles south of town and a mile off the main road, became the nucleus for what later was called "Little Norway." Some of the early settlers there included Jacob Waagbo, Ole Omland, Ed Larsen, Fred Larsen, John Rude, and Sverke Ulvund.

Ole Waagbo lost all interest in his newly acquired property after the tragedy involving Henry and moved to Oregon. He rented the Waagbo farm to Jacob Waagbo, an older brother who had already acquired considerable land in Antrim county, but who needed a home and barn until his own could be built.

Young Jacob Waagbo of central Norway near Trondhjem had been urged by relatives in Michigan to join them. He traveled to Liverpool to await passage to New York. The cheapest boat available to him was a cattle boat. The smelly trip took 18 days. He spent three days getting off the boat in New York and getting ready to travel on. It took so long because there were so many immigrants waiting to pass through Ellis Island.

There was much thievery in all the confusion. Waagbo told the story of how one Norwegian family brought fine silver with them, distributed among all the family members. Before they even passed through immigration every piece had been stolen out of hand, the crowd of immigrants was so large.

Finally, Jacob was put on the proper train which took him to Niagara Falls in Canada. From there he went by boat to Detroit where he met a Norwegian who took him as a traveling companion. This man was very entertaining and Jacob was impressed. After interminable delays and much changing of trains in Michigan, Jacob found himself in Traverse City.

At Traverse City he was told to take one of the boats that sailed daily to Northport. He arrived there late in the evening. Walking away from companionship he went down to the water's edge. Knowing himself to be alone, he took off his dusty, dirty traveling clothes and bathed in the fresh water until he felt clean. He then put on all clean clothes and walked back into the town. Inquiring about his uncle, he ran across a man who promised to take him to his destination.

It was not difficult to find a job, so Waagbo was soon rolling logs and lumber off the train. The pay was only 50 cents a day. He worked on the railroad for

Even at age 81, Jacob Wagbo did not shirk his farm chores. He farmed with draft horses, as shown here, all his life and considered many modern conveniences sinful. *Photo from the Wagbo Peace Center collection.*

a good many months. Later, his uncle took him to Chicago where he learned enough about engineering to become successful at Western Electric.

About this time he met and married Bertha Eide, also from Norway. They went back to Norway on their honeymoon visiting both sets of parents who still lived there in different parts of the country.

Back in Michigan, they rented the home built by Henry Waagbo and then owned by Ole Waagbo, and eventually purchased the property.

The couple became active members of the community and raised three daughters: Anna, Martha and Olga. They replaced the first cabin with a frame home in 1911 and also built a home nearer to the river and town as an investment. When their farm home burned in 1929, the "investment" house was moved to the farm.

About the time the girls were in high school the family decided to drop one "a" from their last name. It seemed more American to them and was easier to pronounce. Jake worked well into his 80s, marking the fields for corn and potatoes, planting, haying, plowing and doing many other farm chores.

My favorite story about Jake Wagbo was told over morning coffee at the Round Table by an old fellow who knew the Wagbos as a youngster: "Jake Wagbo was a different sort of man. He didn't settle matters like most folks would. One night a buddy and I 'visited' his watermelon patch long after dark. We parked near the back of his field and in short order, had the trunk full of those sweet watermelons. As we snuck back to get away, we heard ol' Jake's voice from out of the dark, saying, 'Good night, boys.' We took off like a flash, hopeful that he hadn't identified us. Well, the next night, we couldn't resist going back. When we got to where we had parked the night before, we spied a small sign. It read: One of these watermelons is poisoned. Well, that was enough to turn us around for home!"

It is told that you could go by the Wagbo property any day of the winter and see many people from the Little Norway settlement skiing on the hills. This was a normal part of life in Norway, and although the Jordan Valley doesn't quite match the mountainous landscape of their homeland, it must have sufficed.

There are well-worn cross-country skis still in the Wagbo house that must have seen many a snow covered mile in their day.

After the deaths of her sisters Ann and Olga, Martha left the 212-acre family farm and estate in trust to the Institute for Global Education of Grand Rapids, Michigan. It was Martha's wish that her home to used as a place of education and calm reflection on issues of peace, justice, nonviolent conflict resolution and responsible care of the environment.

Her wish was carried out and today the old Wagbo homestead is operated as the Wagbo Peace Center, non-profit peace education and retreat facility. 🌿

One-room Schools

BY BILL GAUNT

There were five one-room school buildings north of East Jordan in the late 1800s. Most of them were still being used in 1929 when they consolidated with the East Jordan public school district.

These school buildings were built about two miles apart so no child had to walk more than a mile to school, but I am sure it seemed farther than that back then.

The first school in the area was the Star School in School District No. 6. A half acre of land on what is now the corner of Wurn and Loomis Roads about six miles north of East Jordan was bought in 1879 for the school from a Robert Newsen. The front of the school faced north and it was built of rough sawn lumber which was the best you could do at the time unless you were a lumber baron or had a planing mill in your backyard.

An old photograph of the school that I have seen shows about 20 people standing in front of it. They are not identified but were likely members of such families in the area as Bennetts, Russells, Arnetts, Wurns, Haydens and Reichs.

One young man I could identify was Ray Loomis who lived in the neighborhood for many years and left many children and grandchildren. I remember him best as one of the callers for square dances held at the school house every Saturday night for many years. These were truly the good old days; no problems with drugs, fighting or too much booze—just lots of good, clean fun.

The first Star School building burned in about 1903 and was replaced with a new structure that faced east. That is the building that still stands today. It was used as a school during the week and on Sunday for church and Sunday school. Although most of the early records on who taught at the school have been lost, some of the teachers in the 1916 to 1929 period included Marcia Goss, Irene Gunsolas, Beryl McDonald, Frances Pendock, Mabel Zoulek, Frances Gould and Florence Novotny.

After it was consolidated with East Jordan in 1929, the Star School was purchased by a man named Farrs Stone and given to the community. It continued to be used as a church and Sunday school until about 1972. Since then it has been used only occasionally for such activities as Christmas parties and one-room school enactments for local school students.

Another one-room school, the Hillegas School, was located about a mile south of Ridge Road on Wangeman Road. Not much is known about this old school other than the fact it existed from about 1880 to 1890 when it either burned or was closed. The Three Bell School was built to replace it in 1893. Interestingly, records indicate that the Hillegas School was on one acre of land and cost $100 while the Three Bell School was on one and a half acres but cost only $12.58.

The Three Bell School was located about one mile south of the intersection of Ridge and Peninsula Roads. The building is gone now; it was torn down shortly after consolidation. But surviving records identify many families whose children attended the school: Price, Benson, Carslow, Dickie, Crowell, Simmerman, Gaunt, Sandel, McKee, Johnston, Ward, Coblentz, Perry, Healey, Hudson, Lew, Corrothers, Randel, Hott, Turcott, Washburn, LaLond and Lane. Teachers included Ella Barnett, Florence Barret, Vesta Hughson, Nettie Chamberlain, Ruth Emrey, Bertha Jones, Ethel Brintnall, Dorothy McDonald, Mildred Wangeman, Ciccel Ogden, Goldie Summerville and Frances Gould.

Farther north on the peninsula was Mountain School, located on Ferry Road at the north end of what is now Mountain Road. The few surviving records for this school indicate that the land for it was bought on September 3, 1887. In the 1916-17 era, the teacher was Catherine LaLonde and members of the school board were William Howe, George Loomis and W.A. Stanley. Some former students included Oswald Hosegood, Bruce Sanderson, Clare Staley, Marjorie Scott, and Elva, Howard and Nile Gould.

This school building has been turned into the

Eveline Township Hall and has been kept in very good repair.

The last one-room school on the peninsula was Chaddock School, the land for which was purchased in 1882. It was located on the corner of Advance Road and Dutchmans Bay Road about two miles from East Jordan. Hazel Heath was a teacher there in 1916-17 and school board members at the time included J.E. Chew, Mose Hart and Martin Ruhling. Two families that attended were Shepards and Umlors.

Near tragedy at the Opera House

BY W.A. LOVEDAY

In the early 1900s acetylene gas was used for lighting buildings in villages that did not possess municipal electric lighting plants. In the busy northern Michigan lumbering town of East Jordan, the 800-person capacity East Jordan Opera House was fully equipped with this new manner of lighting.

To light such a large building the gas was produced from calcium carbide using a large water sealed generator and storage tank for producing and storing the gas. This setup was installed in the basement and gas was piped throughout the building. The generator worked automatically and was equipped with a safety escape pipe to carry any excess gas out-of-doors after the storage tank was filled.

This lighting system proved very satisfactory in the absence of electricity. One night, however, a large number of patrons were enjoying a stage show when the opera house manager noticed the smell of gas. Without causing any alarm and wishing to avoid a panic, he hastened to the basement and discovered that gas was bubbling up around the water seal of the generator, the safety outlet having gotten clogged, and the automatic dripping of water on the carbide (which produced the gas) continued to operate even though the gas storage tank was full.

The manager had installed many of these lighting plants and instantly recognized the danger of an explosion which might cost many lives unless quick action was taken. Coming back into the theater, he dispatched one of the ushers to get the plumber who had actually installed the lighting plant. At the same time, he sent two or three other ushers to neighboring stores, which were then using gasoline lights for illumination (stores kept open evenings in those days), and borrowed about a half dozen portable lamps to light the building when the acetylene was shut off. The precaution of opening some of the balcony windows was not overlooked.

The plumber arrived within a very few minutes. He and the manager opened the outside basement doors, By that time the generator was almost red hot. They carefully lifted off the water-sealed generator cover, lifted out the heavy pail of hot generating calcium-carbide, weighing close to 100 pounds, and carried it outside and away from the building.

The substitute lighting was accomplished without many of the patrons knowing it, and no one in the building except the manager realized the seriousness of a condition which, without prompt action, might have caused a calamity.

If ever a woman deserved a crown...

BY VIRGINIA KAAKE-GIACOMELLI

It was at a Works Projects Administration (WPA) meeting at the high school in the late 1930s when Dr. Bernard Beuker, East Jordan's long time physician and artist, unveiled his latest painting entitled "The West Side Angel of Mercy." The painting was of a woman with Gypsy-like features: dark eyes and heavy eyebrows, identifiable to many people gathered in the room.

"If ever a woman deserves a crown in heaven," said Dr. Beuker, "It is this woman, Hattie Kaake."

There were nods of agreement throughout the room. To the people who knew her, Hattie Kaake—practical nurse and midwife who delivered dozens of babies and, sometimes years later, helped get them ready for burial—was an angel of mercy.

In an interview in her later years, Hattie told of her work with the people of East Jordan during good times, and the bleaker periods.

"I can remember that, during the Depression, I would go into houses where no one else would go to bring soup and hot loaves of bread, which I would make every day," she said. "Or back in 1918 when the Asian flu epidemic hit East Jordan and people were dying like flies. Dr. Dickens and Dr. Ramsey were the only two doctors we had to take care of an entire community, and the undertaker was as busy as the doctors."

Harriet Kaake. *Photo from the collection of Virginia Kaake-Giacomelli.*

Recalled Hattie's eldest daughter Blanche, "We were kids then and I can still remember watching out the window and seeing Mom going from house to house with the lantern in her hand, night after night, all night long."

"One of the strangest things I can remember," said Hattie, closing her eyes to help her memory, "was going to this one house where the mother was about to have a baby. When I arrived she was lying on the American flag (a new one), the only thing covering the bed."

" 'You can't have a baby on the American flag,' I told the woman. Poor soul, it was all she had that was clean. So I went home and got fresh sheets and blankets. If I wouldn't have done so, it might have been the first baby born on the American flag."

I am the youngest daughter of Harriet ("Hattie") and George Kaake. I was born in 1921 so I do not remember the same things my sisters remember as they were all at least ten years older. I do remember being awakened in the middle of the night many times, hearing "Hattie, come quick; Ethel (or Gladys, Mary, Leda, etc.) is in labor." Mom would grab her bag and cloak and away she would go. Sometimes it was a horse and sled, sometimes a horse and buggy. More often it was on a dead run.

The time of her return home would depend on the condition of the mother and baby. She might bring home a chicken, some vegetables or a piece of beef; but often, nothing. That was her pay and she was always very pleased with herself no matter what way it went.

Irene Brennan told me the Dr. Ramsey used to tell his patients, "If you go into labor, call Hattie. If my services are needed, Hattie will send for me."

My father was Scotch and not as giving as my mother. I would walk in from school and my mom would say, "Take this soup and bread to the Smiths and Blacks (fictional names) as they have nothing to eat. Remember, if your dad asks how many loaves of bread I made, be sure to tell him eight, not ten. The soup I watered down so we are all right there." This happened many times.

For some reason, all the transients who traveled through East Jordan stopped at our house. My mother never turned anyone away. They would have a beat-up Model T with mattresses on top and packed with utensils, bedding, clothes and children. This was in the Depression and people had heard there was work in the area picking apples, cherries and potatoes.

When my dad would get home from the Red Mill, my mother would tell him the tales of woe of the people who stopped. I can remember my dad walking up the Ellsworth road, looking at every sign post and tree. I would catch up to him and ask, "What are you looking for?"

"I can't understand why all the down-and-outers come to our house," he said. "There must be a mark here somewhere." My dad and I looked for that mark for years. We never found it.

Hattie's last public appearance was as the "Queen of Grandvue" on a float in a July 4th parade. The theme was "you're never too old to be a queen." Our family was there with movie cameras. Children were running along calling to their "Aunt Hattie." I know she felt loved like a queen.

The Canning Factory

BY ARVILLA KOWALSKI

The canning factory crew gathered for a group photo, taken sometime in the late 1920s. *Photo from the collection of Virginia Kaake-Giacomelli.*

By the 1920s, East Jordan businessman W.P. Porter realized the need for new industry to replace the dwindling lumber trade which had fueled the growth of East Jordan for so long. The result was a canning factory built as an outgrowth of the existing flooring plant on the bank of the Jordan River. Both plants were operated by the same steam boiler.

Locally grown cherries were the first product to be processed at the canning factory. By 1930 raspberries, beans and beets had been added and in 1935 carrots were introduced.

Production increased yearly. In 1940 the capacity of the plant was 100,000 cans. The warehouse burned in March, 1942 and a new plant was built the same year. Production reached 220,000 cans by 1948.

At that point the plant employed about 250 people for each shift during the peak season. Employees made from 85 cents to a dollar per hour and could earn $500 to $600 a season. The plant also employed 40 to 50 high school students in the summer.

The canning factory used produce grown within a 50-mile radius of East Jordan. When picking began, school buses were used to transport children to the orchards and fields to pick cherries, beans and other vegetables.

The Jordan brand of canned fruits and vegetables were marketed in many states and could be found as far south as Florida and Texas and as far west as Missouri. During World War II, as much as 50 percent of the plant's output was shipped overseas to feed our hungry soldiers.

In 1960, William and Fred Sherman leased the canning factory for one year and in 1961 they bought it. The company was incorporated in 1969 as the Sherman Canning Company and a second generation of Sherman family, William, Robert and Theodore Sherman, joined the management team. In 1971 the firm was producing about 400,000 cans a year.

Sherman Canning continued to increase its level of business by adding new products and expanding production volume. In 1977 the firm entered a joint venture with Traverse City Canning Co. in the acquisition of the Elk Rapids Packing Co. Three years later it became the sole owner of the Elk Rapids plant. Sherman Canning purchased a third processing facility in 1984 in Hartford, Michigan, which handled apple and tomato products.

By 1989, the company's three facilities were processing 70 million pounds of Michigan-grown fruits and vegetables annually with combined sales of over $20 million. In 1988 Elk Rapids Packing and Burnette Foods merged and Burnette Foods has since become the surviving corporate identity for all three plants

which now process cherries, asparagus, green and wax beans, carrots, beets, potatoes and kidney beans.

At the East Jordan plant, modern machinery allows the entire canning operation to be run today by 30

TOP: At one time, East Jordan's canning factory marketed products throughout a good portion of the country under its own label. *Photo from the Portside Art and Historical Museum collection.*

BOTTOM: The canning factory, shown here in 1927, bustled with extra help during the harvest season. *Photo from the collection of Virginia Kaake-Giacomelli.*

people. The plant still markets its products over a widespread area under a number of labels including Shur-Fine, Meijer, Kroger and Oregon.

George Secord: Master storyteller

BY BILL DAVIS

George Secord was an eternal boy, a pixie, a sprite. He was always ready for a trip, a joke or a story. He loved books (especially railroad books), opera, ballet, cats and jazz.

He heard firsthand the sounds of the ancient pines crashing down, the whines of the big mills' saws and the chuffing and whistling of the Detroit & Charlevoix trains bustling about. Most of all he heard the campfire and stovetop stories of lumbermen, railroaders, hangers-on and others. He heard the stories, remembered them and passed them on.

George was a storyteller and what a spectacular event the telling was. With his blue eyes twinkling merrily, his hands flashing around the room, spit flying, teeth clicking and cackling in his enthusiasm, he told and retold the stories. In his telling was the flavor and thrill of being there yourself. George took his listener smack into the heart of history itself.

To fully enjoy one of George's stories, you have to place yourself on a faded and dusty old chaise lounge on George's back porch, a cold drink tinkling in your hand, as you listened:

"Back in 1907, the day before the Fourth of July, the crew of the local freight train had been celebrating a little early with a few drinks. Their cabbage cutter had orders to wait in the hole in Nirvana until the big Mikado hauling the fast freight roared past on its way down to Ludington.

"The boys thought they would play a little joke on one of the town bums so they picked up Bernie Harris and pitched him up on the cow catcher. They figured they would have time to pop out on the main track, race up to Oliver's Station, and duck in the siding there to let the fast freight fly on past.

"So they all jumped on the cabbage cutter with Bernie propped up on the cow catcher, put the coal to her and chugged on up the grade, scorching the ballast.

"Just over the horizon, inevitable as doom, the big westbound fast freight came, piling on just east of Clemenshaw's Crossing. That big Mikado came roaring down around one end of the S curve and the cabbage cutter came chuffing up around the other end.

Both crews saw what was happening in time and joined the birds just before the locomotives hit head on in a real cornfield meet.When the dust settled and the hissing steam cleared they dug through the wreckage and found Bernie. There wasn't a scratch on him but he was dead. Might have woke up and died of fright. Poor Bernie, he likely never knew how he came to join the angels."

George also recalled the Venezuela, or "the Venzie," a huge wooden hulled lake freighter that would come down the South Arm riding low in the water, all bunkers topped off with iron ore from Escanaba. She would give long blasts on her whistle as if Gabriel had sounded his horn and all the brawny young farm boys anxious for a cash money job would pile down from the haylofts and race down to the foundry docks to hire on. They would check out their shovels and, working 12-hour shifts, sling the iron ore up and out into the tram cars to be trundled up to the foundry smelter.

George loved to tell about his favorite railroad, the Pere Marquette, and his favorite train on it, the Resort Special. It was 14 pullman cars long, sleepers up from Cincinnati, Louisville, Indianapolis, St. Louis and Chicago every summer evening, whistling over the hills as its "good ol' gal", a big Pacific, rolled it down into Charlevoix before the run up to Petoskey.

In his last summer, George took me up to Petoskey to meet his lifelong love, a woman whose pigtails he had dunked often in his desk's ink well in grade school. The stories started and she told of her long ago trip on the East Jordan and Southern when a redheaded conductor named Mr. Sweet stopped the train between Marble and Mt. Bliss to climb off and gather a bunch of arbutus for her.

Ah, what a sweet man George was. He drank deeply from the rich cup of life. Now his ashes are mixed with the old dune north of East Jordan above the lake. The cemetery sexton knows exactly where they are, next to his Mabel, his beloved mother. If the whistles are ever heard again of the old wooden steamers coming up the lake, or the steam locomotives charging through the valley, George is in perfect position to hear.